g AUTUMN 2024
NUMBER 34

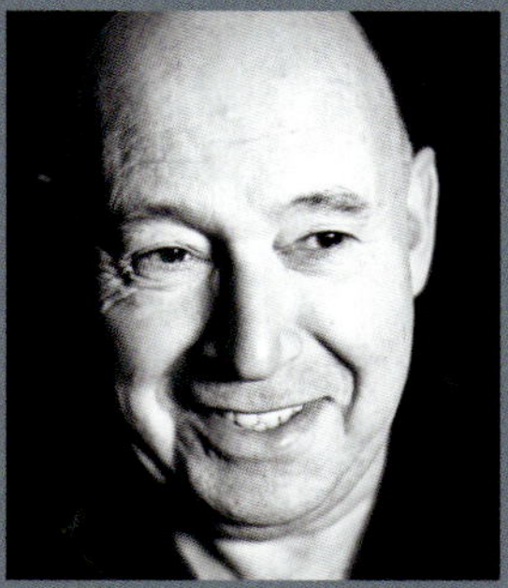

This Autumn issue arrives at a bittersweet moment for us at the gallery. The past few weeks have seen the loss of two artists with whom we have been working closely in recent months. Graham Boyd, who was 96 – and still painting every day – had an enthusiasm for art, paint and colour that was wonderfully infectious. Over a 70-year career he never stopped exploring where his vibrant abstractions might take him. We will remember his unending energy with a celebratory exhibition later this October.

It was an extraordinary series of events that saw us reunited with Norman Ackroyd earlier this year, three decades after we had last worked together. That chance meeting subsequently sparked the completion of another exceptional project of Norman's that had lain dormant for years. I am delighted that we have been able to bring it to fruition – and deeply saddened that Norman, who passed away on the 16th September, just days after the last details were finalised, won't be here to celebrate it with us. However, for both artists, the work lives on and continues to bring joy, as I hope the other fantastic features in this magazine will too.

Mike

Words: Max Waterhouse
Except pages: 6 © Ceri Levy
60 © Mark Haddon
62 © Julian Spalding
Photographs: Jay Goldmark, Christian Soro, Vicki Uttley
Design: Porter/Waterhouse, October 2024
Printed in Wales by Gomer Press

ISBN 978-1-915188-23-6

CONTRIBUTORS

Ceri Levy is a filmmaker, writer, and 'gonzovationist'. As a creator of many music videos and documentaries, he is best known for his 2009 film *Bananaz*, following the cartoon-band Gorillaz. With the artist Ralph Steadman he co-authored the successful Gonzovation Trilogy of books, comprising *Extinct Boids*, *Nextinction* and *Critical Critters*. In 2006, Levy was invited to film the process of Norman Ackroyd's *Alchemy on Anglesey*, a project that aimed to produce a series of etchings of Anglesey on plates of copper mined from the island itself.

Mark Haddon is a writer and artist, widely celebrated as the author of the bestselling novel *The Curious Incident of the Dog in the Night-Time*, for which he was awarded the Whitbread Award. His latest book, *Dogs and Monsters*, Haddon's second collection of short stories, was published by Chatto & Windus in August of this year.

Julian Spalding is an art historian, writer, broadcaster and a former curator. An outspoken critic of the art world, he has frequently contributed to arts, news and current affairs programmes on radio and TV. Spalding was one of Francis Davison's first critical champions, curating the artist's sole lifetime retrospective at the Hayward Gallery, 1983. A fuller account of his friendship with Davison, the development of his work, and its unlikely impact on Damien Hirst appears in his professional memoir *Art Exposed* (Pallas Athena, 2023).

goldmark
Orange Street, Uppingham, Rutland
LE15 9SQ 01572 821424
info@goldmarkart.com
www.goldmarkart.com

Contents

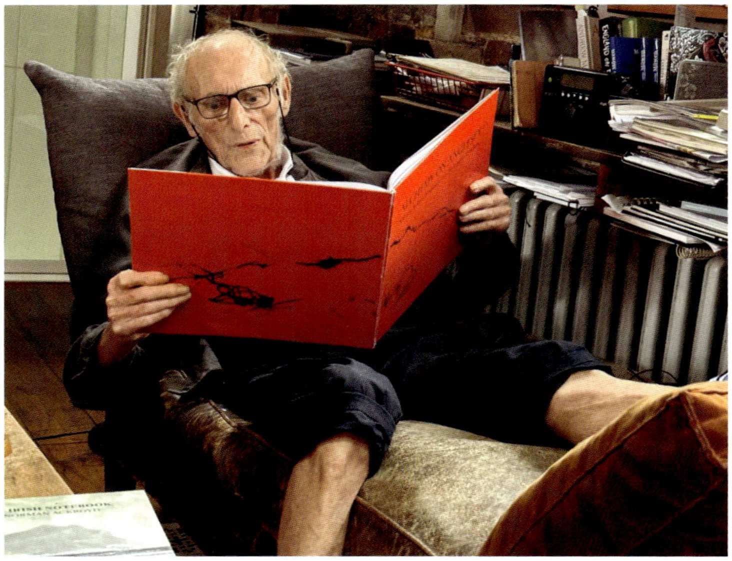

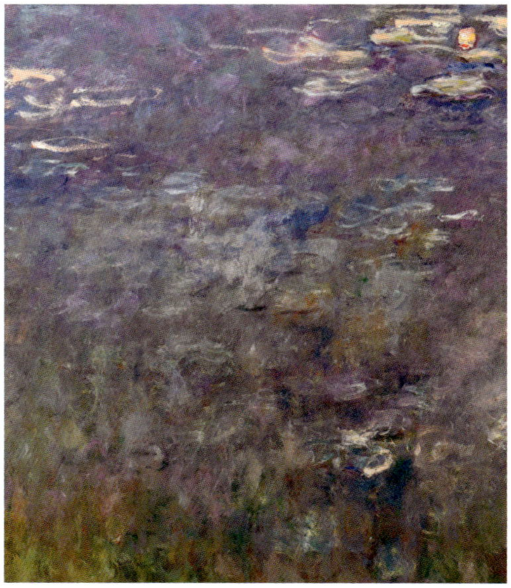

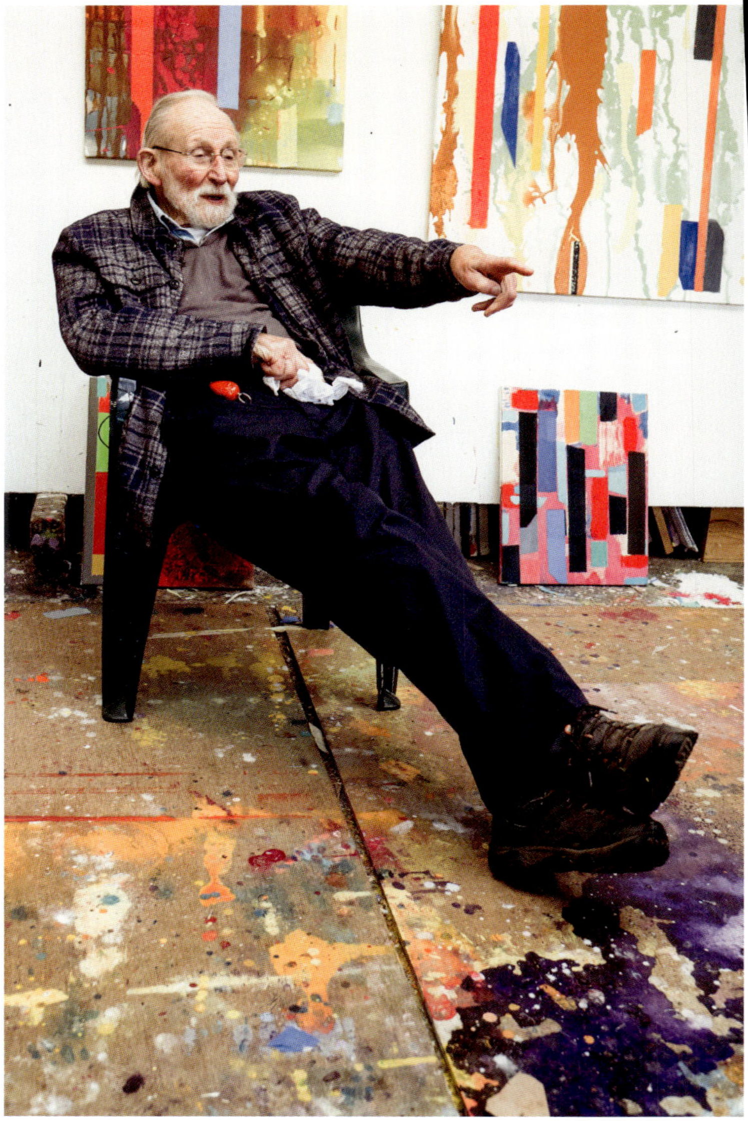

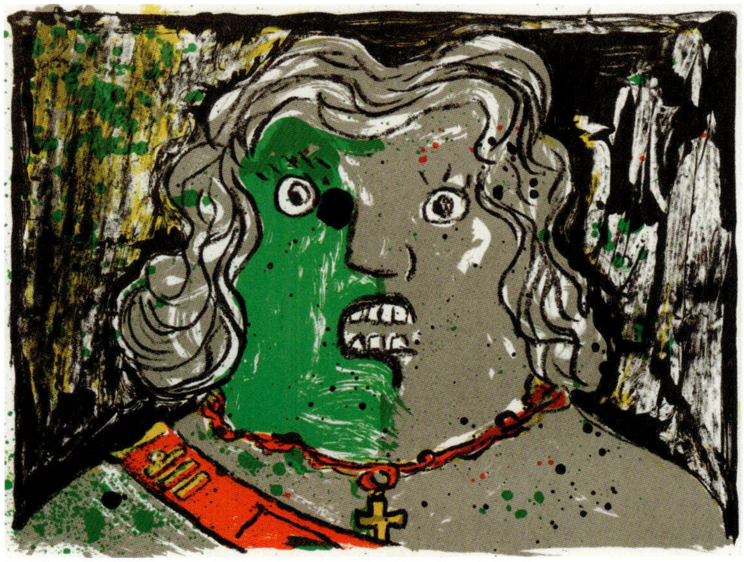

30. Enrico Baj: Enfant Terrible

When the young Milanese artist Enrico Baj announced the arrival of his 'Nuclear Art' movement in 1951, he declared there would be no future use for academic 'isms' or pretty geometries. He dedicated the rest of his career instead to a brash and animated savaging of political corruption, fabricating paintings and prints with scrappy materials and inventing an irreverent iconography that soon attracted the ire of Italian censors.

40. Leonard Baskin, The Native American Portraits

In 1968, with tensions sharply rising in the Vietnam War, the sculptor and printmaker Leonard Baskin was tasked with commemorating a much older conflict: the doomed charge of General Custer against Sioux and Cheyenne tribes at the Battle of Little Bighorn. The results were among his strongest drawings to date – and seeded a fascination that would last over 30 years.

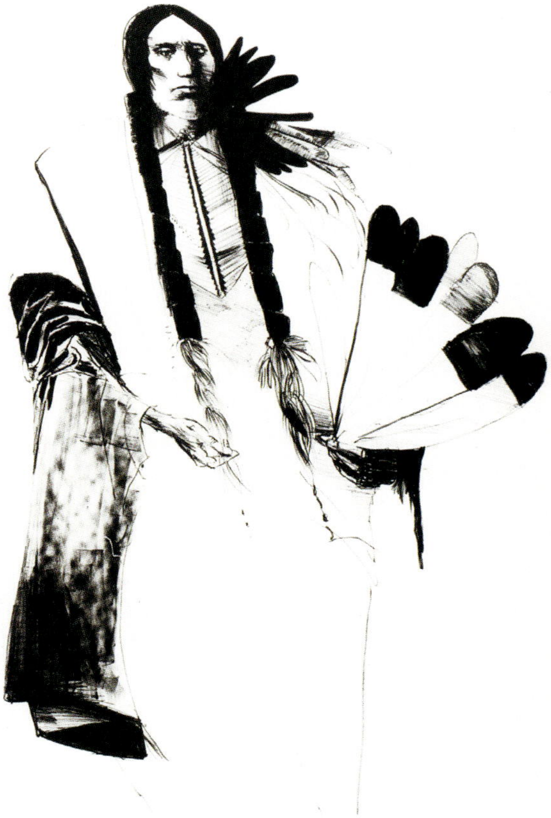

50. Colours by Number: Rothenstein's Red

An idyllic childhood in the Stroud Valley introduced the young Michael Rothenstein to a world of natural splendour and farmyard violence. Decades later, the drawings he made in his formative years continued to inform his work in print – most especially, their vibrant vermillion red palette.

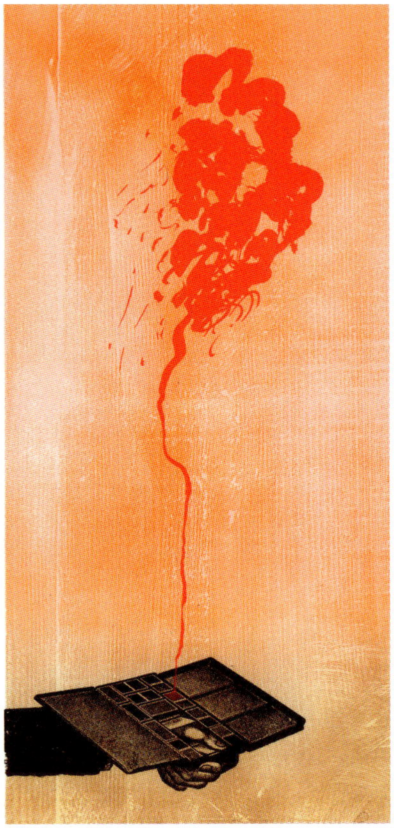

57. HIGHLIGHTS

- Julian Spalding illuminates the paper collages of Francis Davison
- Mark Haddon on the unrestrained joy of French potter Jean-Nicolas Gérard
- And rare Picasso woodcuts join works by Eileen Cooper, Mary Fedden and Anne Mette Hjortshøj & more in our latest gallery arrivals

ALCHEMY ON ANGLESEY

Norman Ackroyd's Journey Into The Copper Kingdom

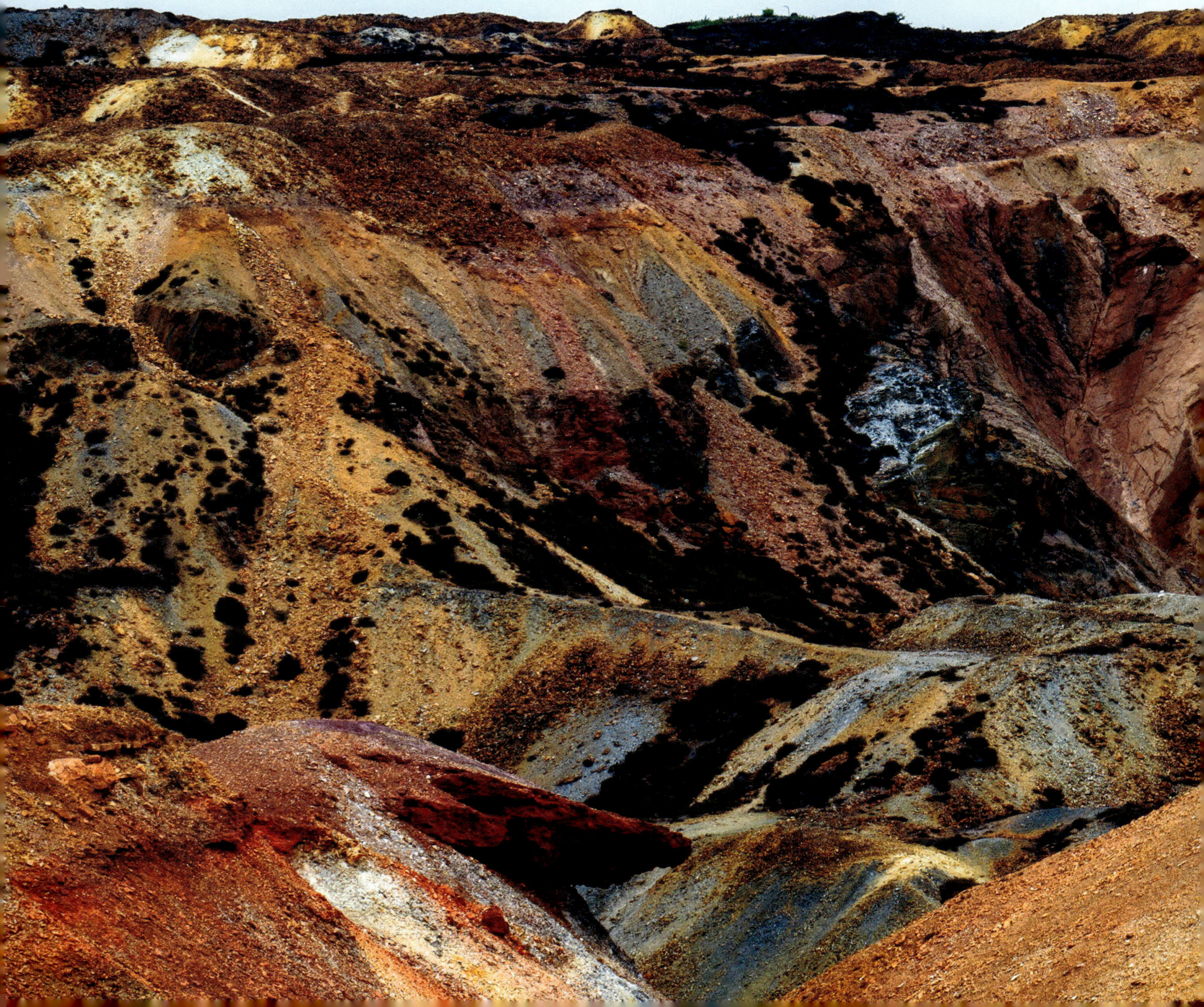

For years Norman Ackroyd (1938-2024) immortalised the British Isles in his brooding aquatints. **Ceri Levy** *details the genesis of his last project – an epic 18 years in the making.*

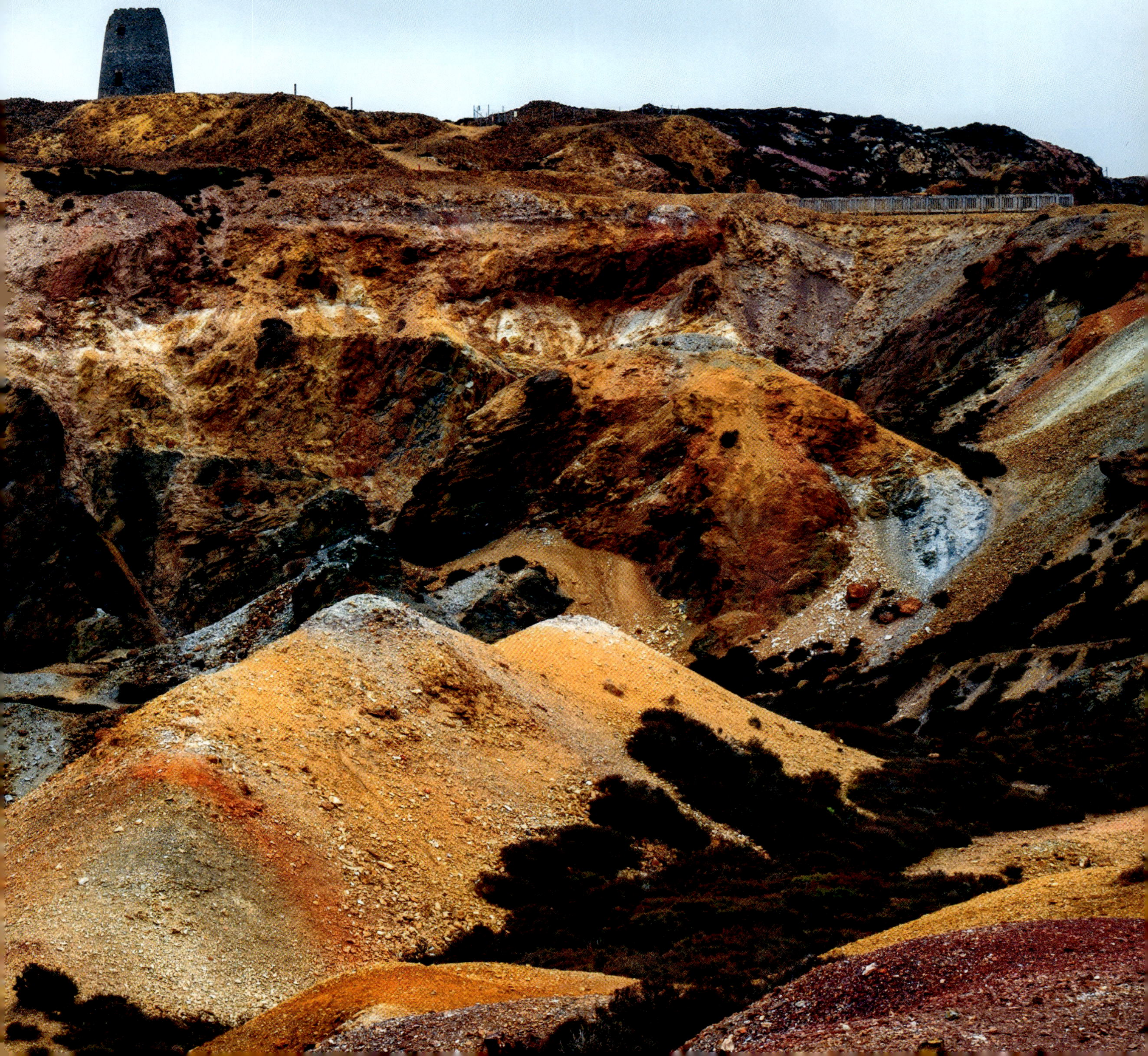

It is with very mixed emotions that I sit here and reflect on Norman Ackroyd's three etchings of Anglesey. Delight that after 18 years, with Norman's encouragement, we have been able to complete this amazing project. And huge sadness to know that he had passed away on the 16th September, just days after its last details were finalised.

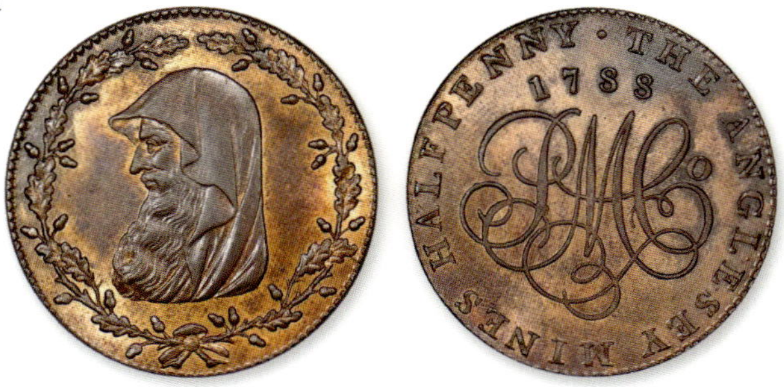

This adventure has been a lesson in alchemy. Ideas into reality. Rocks into copper. Copper into plates. A transformation of time. At last, the magic has worked, and Alchemy on Anglesey can now be revealed.

So how did we get here? Well, let's roll back the clock and I'll tell you…

2008

Robert Kennan, an old friend of mine and now Head of Modern and Contemporary Editions at Phillips, London, approaches me with an idea that he has been working on.

Hi Ceri,

Back in 2006 Norman Ackroyd held a retrospective of his prints at Central Saint Martins College of Art and Design. There was a map, and every location NA had visited on the British Isles coastline was marked with a red dot. Noticing the omission of a dot on Anglesey set me thinking about commissioning a print from Norman.

Last summer staying at our cottage on Anglesey I discovered that there is a copper mine on the island called Parys Mountain. The mine was one of the largest in its heyday and made Amlwch, the local port, the second most important town in Wales during the late 18th and early 19th centuries.

As copper is used for etching plates, I approached NA with the idea of making an etching on copper from Anglesey. He was interested. Sadly, the mine is presently not in operation, so I was stumped as to where to find Anglesey copper.

I had heard that the hulls of Nelson's fleet were sheathed in copper from the mines. The copper prevents "stuff" growing on the hull, slowing the ship down. With a copper lined hull, they moved more quickly through the water and it is said that this assisted Nelson's victory over the French at Trafalgar. I contacted the salvage company who recently stripped the copper from the hull of HMS Victory and produced ingots of copper. Sadly, the ship was re-sheathed in late C19th in copper from Sweden.

By chance, my Nain (Grandmother) gave me a very worn coin and asked me to find out what it was. On one side there was a trace of a profile. Visiting Parys Mine, the signage/logo, for what is now a heritage site (runner up in the Restoration programme on BBC 2), was a coin with the profile of a Druid's head.

The coin was a copper penny, and as I discovered, was a token used to pay workers at the mine. The Druid Head token is regarded as one the finest of its kind and millions were made between 1780 and 1800, a great many by Matthew Boulton at his Soho Foundry in Birmingham. Boulton was a giant of the Industrial Revolution.

The Druid was used because of Anglesey's rich Druid tradition and that the owner of the mine, Thomas Williams, known as The Copper King, lived on the site of the last stand by the Druids against the Romans.

So, find a load of worn Druid tokens, melt them down and make a plate. I do have reservations about melting the coins down, however, they are the only source of copper that was made from ore mined at Parys Mountain that I have found so far.

I took the coins to Henry Abercrombie and the AB foundry who said he could produce an etching plate for Norman. He also said that he was able to make a plate from ore found on Parys Mountain.

So, Norman is going up to Anglesey in a couple of weeks to do some research, and I'm making a copper plate, out of some old coins or boot full of rubble... Chatting with Norman, he thought the whole project had potential to be made into a film and should be documented.

Roll the credits!!

Cheers,
Rob.

The fire has ignited… I have no hesitation in getting involved.

2009

Rob and I visit Anglesey to find copper to make the plates for Norman to etch upon. Rob has bought a large amount of work tokens but thinks it would be great to find some rocks in the mine and turn them into copper. And so, on a cold and wet day we finally disappear into Parys mine with Dave Jenkins, from the Heritage Centre and Dave Chapman, a historian of the area, and collect rocks to burn in a modern version of a Bronze Age smelting pit back at Chapman's studio in his old church. He also gives us some extra pieces of Anglesey copper, comprising the lightning rod from his church and remarkably some sheets of original copper from the hull of the HMS Victory, Nelson's boat at Trafalgar.

The anticipation of what will be removed from the fire is palpable. When, after two days' work, we are ready to discover the fruits of our labours, we open the pit and the transformation is revealed. It is true alchemy as we are left with small beads of copper. It may not be much but the symbolism of the moment as our rocks have turned into shiny copper is exhilarating. Thank God I wasn't around in the Gold Rush! This Copper Buzz is more than we can take.

Rob takes the collection of Anglesey copper to AB Foundry in the East End of London and the pour is made into the casts for the plates. Norman comes along and breaks open the casts to reveal the newly formed copper plates. They will be sent to be polished and then we will all move up to Anglesey for the next stage in the process.

Previous page: The coloured landscape of the disused opencast copper mine on the island of Anglesey in Northern Wales. Photo Shawn Williams/Alamy
Opposite: Copper halfpenny work token from the Parys Mountain mine on Anglesey, 1788
Below: Norman Ackroyd, *The Great Open Cast*, etching

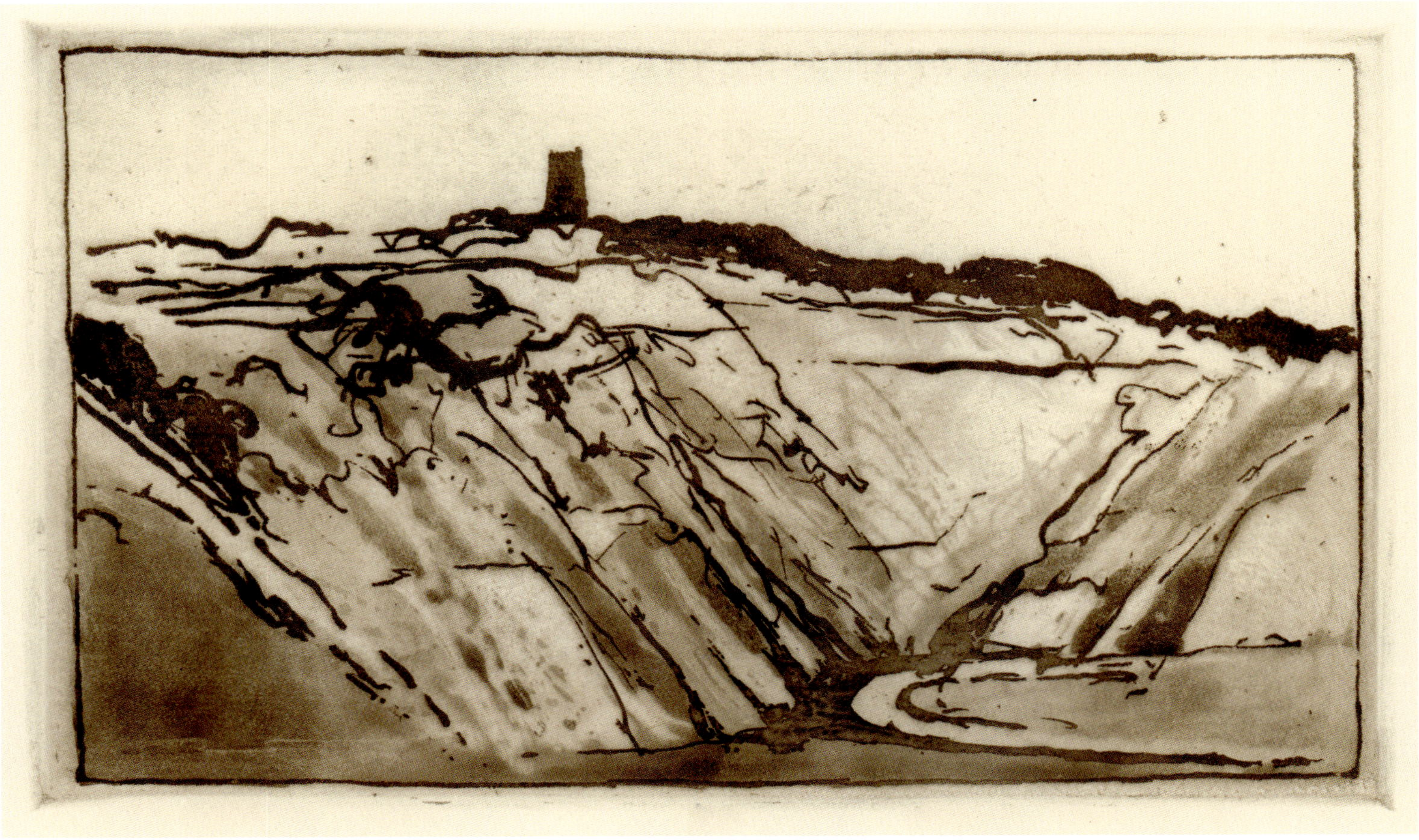

'It's what Francis Bacon called, the "grin without the cat." You want to get something that is really the essence of the place...'

At the Pearl Engine House, Norman stands in the rain mulling over the place to work from. Once decided, he paints a watercolour sketch before working on a plate for an etching. It's as if he is making friends with the world around him and beginning to absorb the place as he connects with it through each brushstroke. He creates a union between himself and the landscape.

Oblivious to the persistent Anglesey wind and rain, he uses the water pooling at his feet to clean his brushes. Watching him switch to working on the recently made copper plates is enthralling. There is a resolve in everything he does. His process is an old companion, and I feel privileged that he reveals so much of himself to us. He is in a near meditative state as he searches for the 'grin without the cat.' He lays down the lines that he sees as the future of this project, working with an intense fluidity, impervious to the downpours as he continues to work until he throws the plate on the ground. He has finished and the sun comes out. Perhaps in honour of his commitment to his work.

Back in London Norman works on the prints but the thickness of the Anglesey copper plates threatens to irreparably damage his press. A few impressions are pulled, but the work grinds to a halt.

Time passes... The project has lost impetus and gradually becomes a distant memory. An unsatisfactory ending to an unfulfilled endeavour. Have our hopes been dashed forever?

Opposite right: Norman Ackroyd, *Amlwch*, etching
Below: Norman Ackroyd, *Pearl Engine House*, watercolour & ink from sketchbook

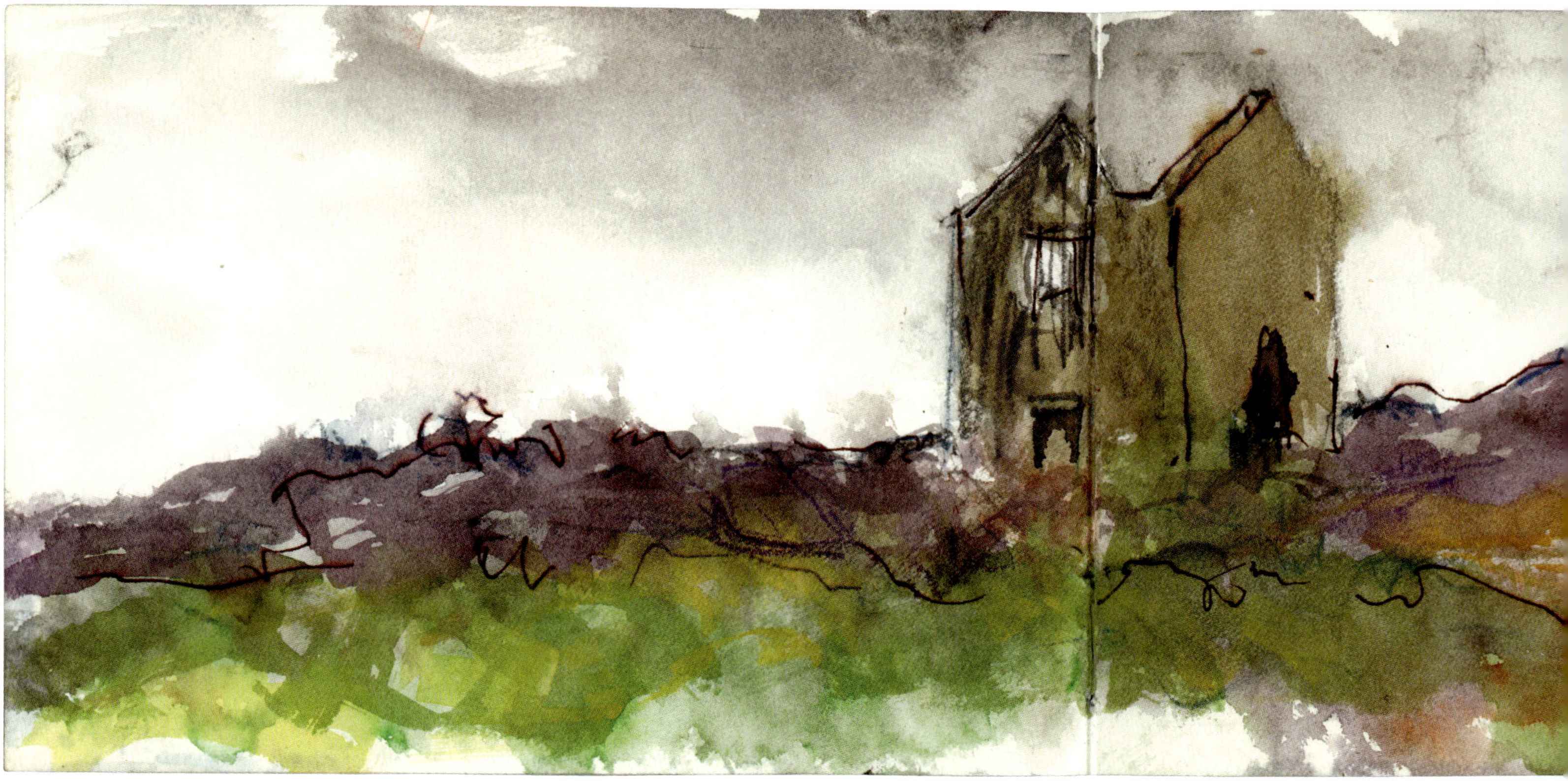

2024

Goldmark Gallery releases its spring magazine, and I see that Norman is featured in it. It takes a moment, but the cogs begin to whir and I pop in to see Mike. I tell him the story of everything that has gone before, and one thing leads to another. New life is breathed back into the Anglesey project.

The Goldmark team move into action and come up with fresh ideas to create an object of beauty. Their master printer, Ian Wilkinson, discovers that the plates need a device to hold them in place due to their thickness. It is a laborious process, and each image must be managed carefully as the press is used. After several weeks of work the edition is finished, Norman is delighted with the results, and this writing is the last thing to be added to the collection of ideas, people, places, objects, materials that have made Norman Ackroyd's Alchemy on Anglesey a reality.

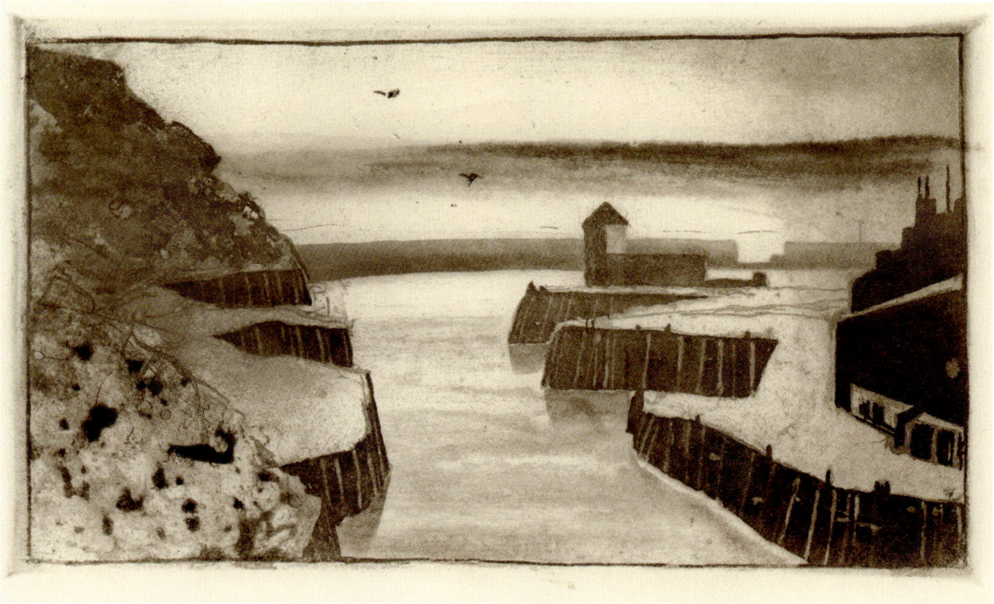

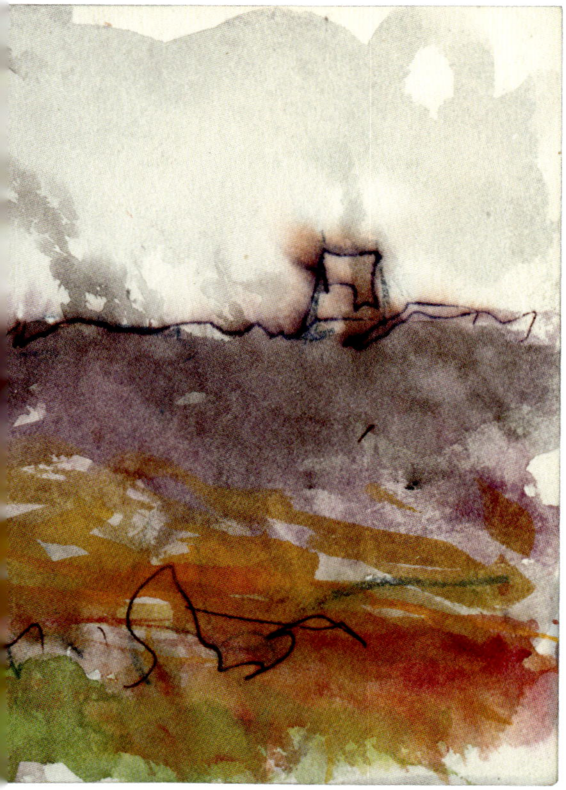

What we have are haunting images of a landscape that once was so different. Amlwch Harbour had been teeming with boats transporting copper to all parts of the world; the Pearl Engine House, built in 1816, pumped water from the mine and pumped it to other engines uphill; the windmill pictured in the Great Open Cast, was built in 1878 to assist a steam engine in pumping and winding and was the first five-sailed structure of its kind in Anglesey. It was closed in 1904 when work at the mine stopped. Now the derelict windmill stands guard over the once precious copper mine. One imagines what the mine looked like back then.

Questions pop into my head as I look at the images. Do people always leave the landscape they find themselves in? Do we lose interest once we have removed that which we deem is of value? What should our relationship be with the world around us? These prints conjure up thoughts of the effects of humanity even though no human is in view.

The echoes of the past resonate through Norman's work. And now these images have been revived, revitalised and brought back to life, we can finally present the finite transformation with this realisation of The Alchemy on Anglesey – Norman Ackroyd's Journey into the Copper Kingdom.

'There is a resolve in everything he does. His process is an old companion, and I feel privileged that he reveals so much of himself to us.'

ALCHEMY ON ANGLESEY

Norman Ackroyd's Journey into the Copper Kingdom

Three original signed and numbered etchings
in a 32pp cloth covered hardback book.
Limited to 75 copies, with 9 APs.

Each book is accompanied by
an c18th Parys mountain copper work token
& a fragment of copper from the hull of
Nelson's HMS Victory.

Special launch price £2,250 (regular price £2,750)

To secure your copy

Phone us on 01572 821424 or email info@goldmarkart.com

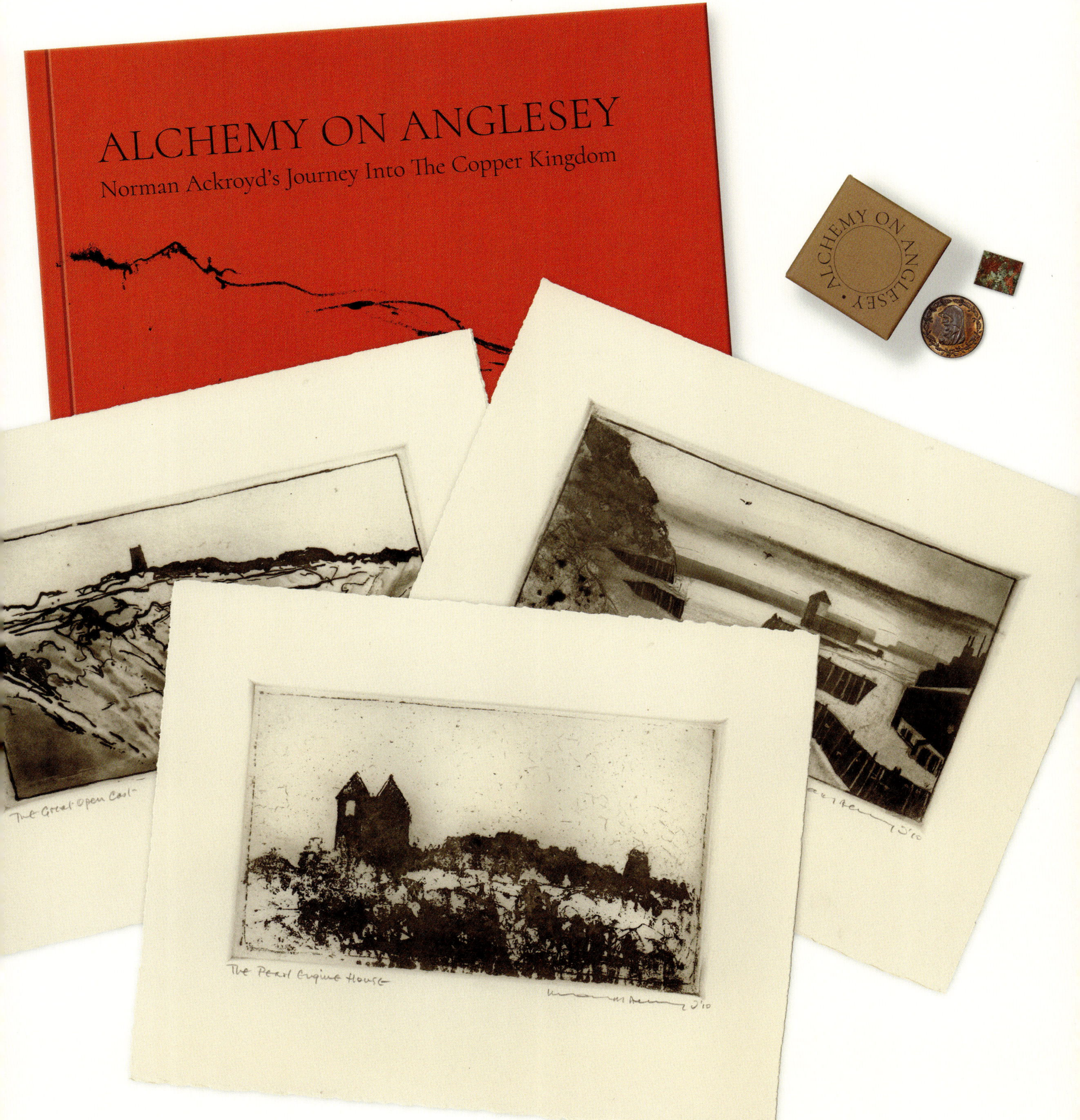
ALCHEMY ON ANGLESEY
Norman Ackroyd's Journey Into The Copper Kingdom
ALCHEMY ON ANGLESEY
The Great Open Cast
The Pearl Engine House

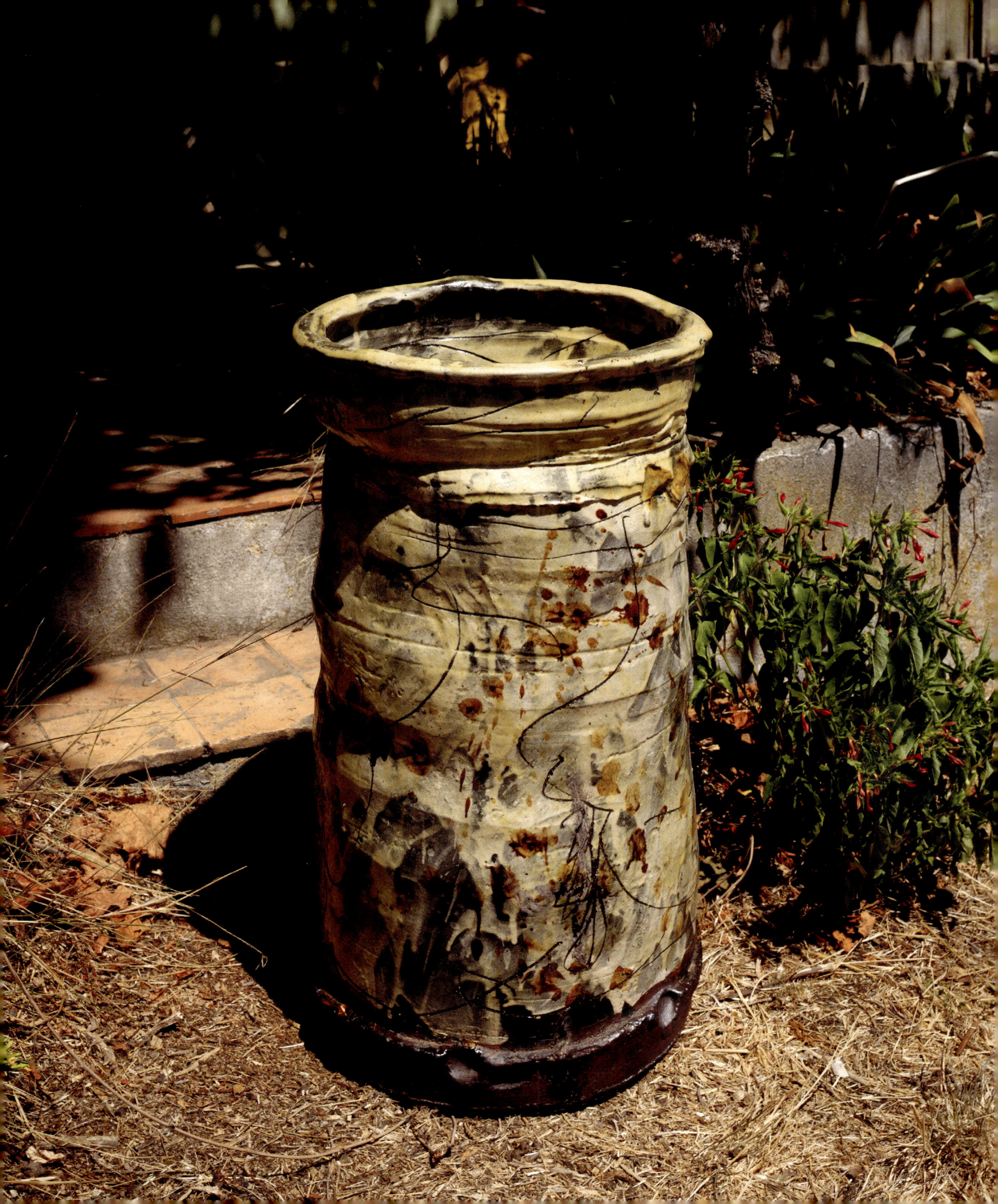

More than Meets the Eye

A gallery encounter prompts reflections from our editor on failing sight and revelations of touch

Earlier this summer, two visitors to the Goldmark Gallery wandered through the low-ceilinged alcove into the small annex space where I work, surrounded, usually, by a hodgepodge curation of prints and the occasional pot. As they walked past me, I noticed that the man was blind: in his left hand he held a cane, and in his right his wife's fingers as she led him through the room. Stopping before each wall, she would narrate what was in front of her. She chose her words carefully, slowly and quite deliberately painting a picture of the shapes and colours that she saw. Rounding a corner, she recognised a large, tall slipware vase by the French potter Jean-Nicolas Gérard; it transpired she, and perhaps her husband too, were amateur potters. Placing his hand on the pot's unglazed rim she slid her fingers between his, so that they could survey it in unison. 'It's a beautiful colour,' she whispered: 'a golden, sunny yellow, dotted with blue and brown spots. Can you feel his thumbprints in the clay?'

I wondered, in that moment, how his imagination might reconcile these contrasts: this warm colour, like the glow of the sun, with the cool surface of the pot itself. Did he have memories of the colours his wife was describing? Were they forever tied to some former object? Were they perhaps clouded, formless? Could he visualise them? Or had the colour yellow always remained for him an elusive abstraction?

Few visually impaired people, I have since learnt, are congenitally blind: most retain a dimmed, narrowed or scattered experience of bright lights and colours. Blindness, for this gentleman, had apparently closed one door of perception, but in doing so seemed to have opened others. What might it mean to experience colour in this purely abstract way? And how much richer could our experience of art be if we remembered to engage our other senses: smells, sound, and most of all touch. Fingers, we forget, can reach round forms to the far side of sight, or follow where light cannot, inside the dark interior of a pot. We can touch as sequentially or as embracingly as we can see, eyes darting around or stepping back to take in the fuller picture. Fingers can trace at one moment and envelope at the next, processing texture, temperature, grain, contour, all at once – things our eyes can only guess at.

I remember my own sight swiftly deteriorating at a young age. At 7 or 8, the changes were imperceptible. Then suddenly, at 9 and 10, words on the classroom whiteboard began to swim and eventually disappear into a haze. I had my first pair of glasses at 11, and realised, as I slid them over my nose, that I had no memory of the world in such clarity. Driving home from the opticians, I stared out the window and saw, for the first time, the distinct shapes of individual leaves on the trees. I had

Jean-Nicolas Gérard, *Very Large Jar*, yellow with brown splashes & sgraffito

presumed – to my mother's distress, when I told her – that everyone experienced car travel as an impressionistic blur.

On the myopic scale, from a low -1 to a severe -10, my prescription has surpassed an 'extreme' -7. Between glasses and daily contact lenses, it's rare now that I spend any great deal of time in my natural state of poor-sightedness. So there was something strangely moving about this episode, watching two people feel their way around the gallery with their hands and their words. When they left, I took out my lenses to experience the world as if I were that little boy again, lost in a wordless room.

With no sight correction, I can determine very little detail in pictures. Even the frame of a painting is so blurred that the picture within it seems almost to settle on the same plane as the wall behind it, its edges fraying like a reflection in water. Colours, by fuzzy displacement into and over one another, take on an ambient temperature; I become aware of hot lights, cool shadows, areas of intensity. Sight itself becomes a kind of tactile response: trying to discern and define the limits and volumes of objects in space, like feeling with the eyes, extending long, invisible fingers as one might grope in a pitch black room with outstretched hands.

In the collection of the Musée d'Orsay there is a wonderful portrait of the artist Claude Monet, perhaps the most famously sight-impaired artist, standing in his garden in Giverny. The photograph itself is a rare example of an 'autochrome', an early colour process that mirrored Monet's own Impressionist techniques: a glass plate is coated in a mosaic of tiny red, blue and green-dyed starch grains that operate as a kind of colour filter for the resulting negative. Somewhat ironically in this example, it is the foreground flowers that stand in sharpest focus. Monet himself resembles a dissolving puff of smoke from his favourite Caporal cigarettes, which friends recalled would climb and wrap itself around him, as vines around a branch.

The date is 1921, five years before his death at the age of 86, and 18 months before he underwent his first surgery to remove the cataract from his right eye, no doubt responsible for his inclination toward hot reds and yellows and pungent browns in paintings of recent years. His eyesight had been declining for decades at this point. Three years earlier, he had voiced the frustrations he had been living with for some time:

> 'I no longer perceived colours with the same intensity, I no longer painted light with the same accuracy. Reds appeared muddy to me, pinks insipid, and the intermediate or lower tones escaped me. As for forms, they always appeared clear and I rendered them with the same decision.
>
> At first I tried to be stubborn. How many times, near the little bridge where we are now, have I stayed for hours under the harshest sun sitting on my campstool, in the shade of my parasol, forcing myself to resume my interrupted task and recapture the freshness that had disappeared from my palette. Wasted efforts. What I painted was more and more dark, more and more like an "old picture," and when the attempt was over and I compared it to former works, I would be seized by a frantic rage and slash all my canvases with my penknife.'

This quote appears in a 1985 article by Dr James G. Ravin, an ophthalmologist based in Toledo, Ohio. In his research, Dr Ravin had been given access to Monet's glasses, his correspondence with his eye surgeon, and even interviewed one of the surgeon's assistants, who was then still alive. The story is one of desperation. Unable to faithfully discern one paint from another by colour alone, Monet was forced instead to organise his palette into a strict order of pigments, deciphered not by sight but from the wording on their tubes.

There was a further complicating factor at play. Several years earlier, Monet had promised a number of vast and, as yet unfinished, water lily paintings as a gift to France. Prime minister Georges Clemenceau, who had negotiated the gift, felt there was little more he could do to them in such circumstances and urged him to have the surgery. Monet, however, had his doubts. He knew Daumier's cataract operation had failed. Mary Cassatt, whose cataracts were diagnosed by Degas' eye doctor, saw no improvement. 'Nothing takes it out of one like painting,' she wrote to a friend. 'I have only to look around me to see that – to see Degas a mere wreck, and Renoir and Monet too.' There were precedents, of course: Titian, Rembrandt, Goya, Turner – all likely suffered degenerating sight. And he certainly wouldn't be the last. Georgia O'Keefe took to pottery when her eyesight failed her in the 1970s, under the influence of her younger companion Juan Hamilton, whose pregnant forms echo O'Keefe's paintings of clouds in New Mexico skies. Prunella Clough described how her thick spectacles, often covered in the grease of inks and oil paints, contributed to her industrial vision. After having her own cataracts removed, she would sit and stare at the blue flame of her gas hob, delighting in a spectrum of light that had been dulled for years.

The perennially anxious Monet took his convalescence less well. His step-son, Jean-Pierre Hoschedé, described how he was first made to lie for days in total darkness, his head sand-bagged to prevent it from moving. When he was eventually allowed to return home to Giverny, he despaired his sight would never recover. The removal of the cataract had left him, Dr Ravin explained, with severe colour discrepancies between his

Claude Monet in front of his house in Giverny, autochrome, 1921, © Musée d'Orsay

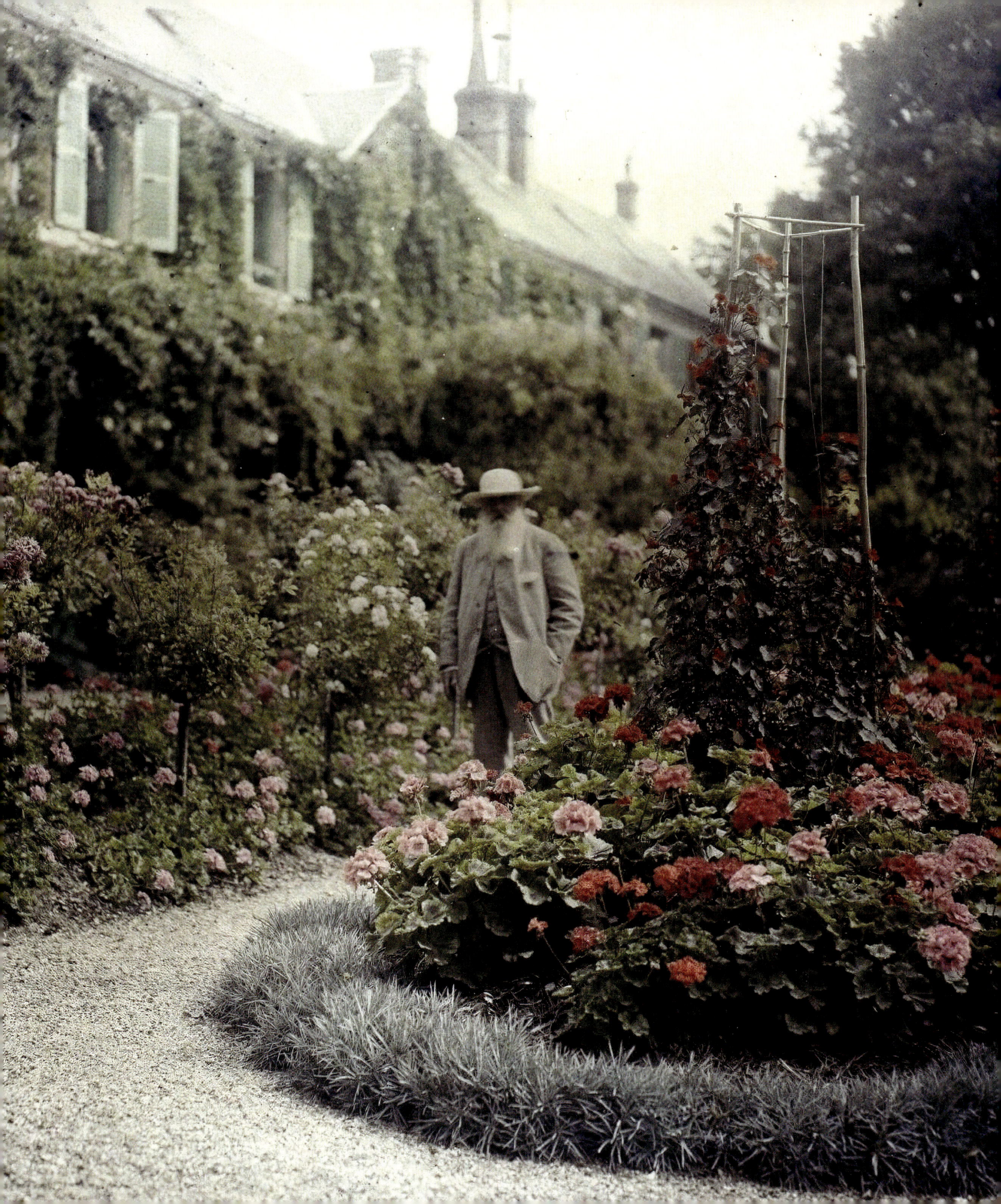

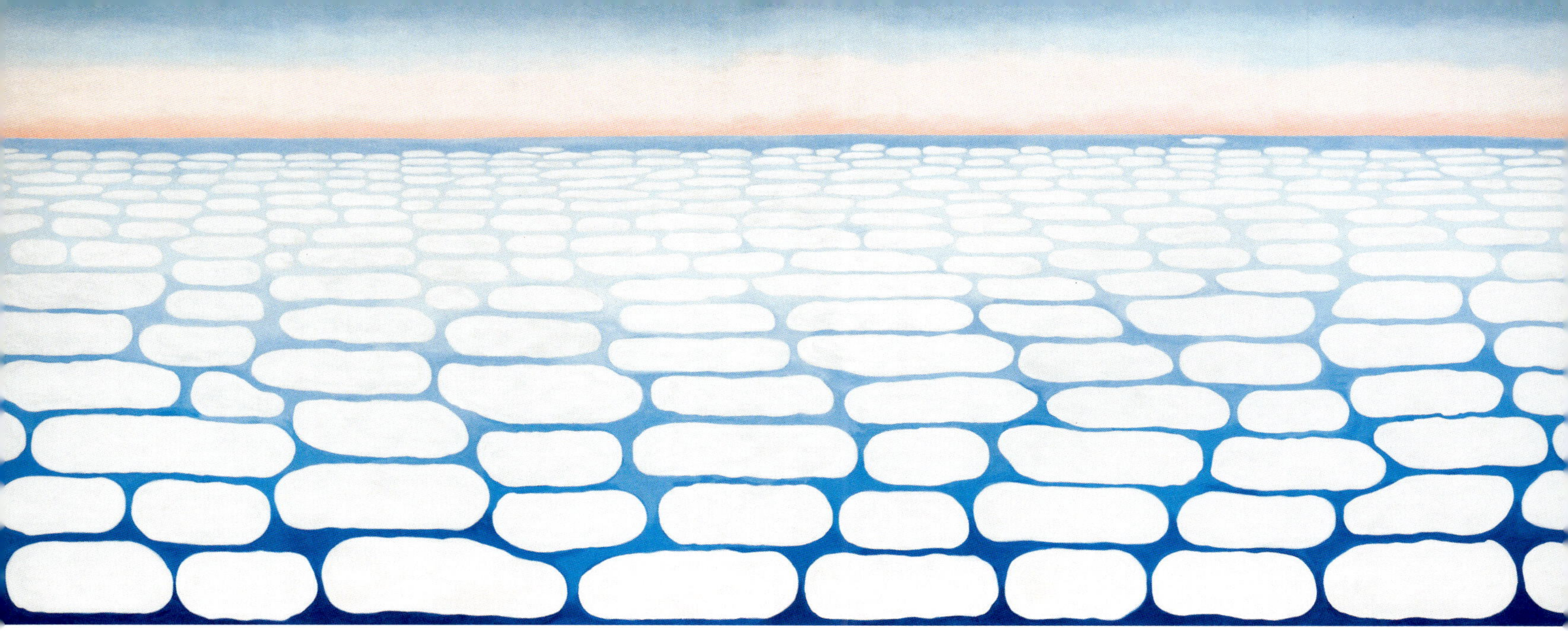

eyes. Cataracts produce a dirty yellow-brown filter in the lens. When this was removed from the right eye, Monet found he could suddenly see the full gamut of blue and violet tones that clashed with what little yellow-tinted sight remained in his left. His corrective glasses strained his vision; he suffered from spherical and chromatic aberrations – objects appearing unnaturally warped and miscoloured. To avoid these violent contrasts, he would use only one eye at a time, occluding the other with a darkened lens or an improvised paper eye-patch, further affecting the perspective of his canvases in the process. Which eye, after all, represented his 'proper' vision? Which colour sense was right?

There is a popular myth, born of the famously bad eyesight of the 'wrecks' Degas, Renoir and Monet, that Impressionism was simply the blur of what they saw. This revisionist history, in which Monet slavishly described exactly what his ailing eyes perceived, misunderstands the very nature of visual art. Painting, Picasso is supposed to have said, is 'a blind man's profession': we bring to pictures what we see, what we feel, and what we know of what is in front of us. Art happens in the space between all three.

What is it, then, that attracts so many to the medicalisation of painting? Dr Ravin's account provides invaluable insight: into the particular challenges Monet faced; the disorientation any artist experiences when their vision is altered, however slowly or suddenly; how all artists as concerned with colour as Monet was must reckon with the disparity between seeing and feeling. But the appeal of this kind of insight stems from the

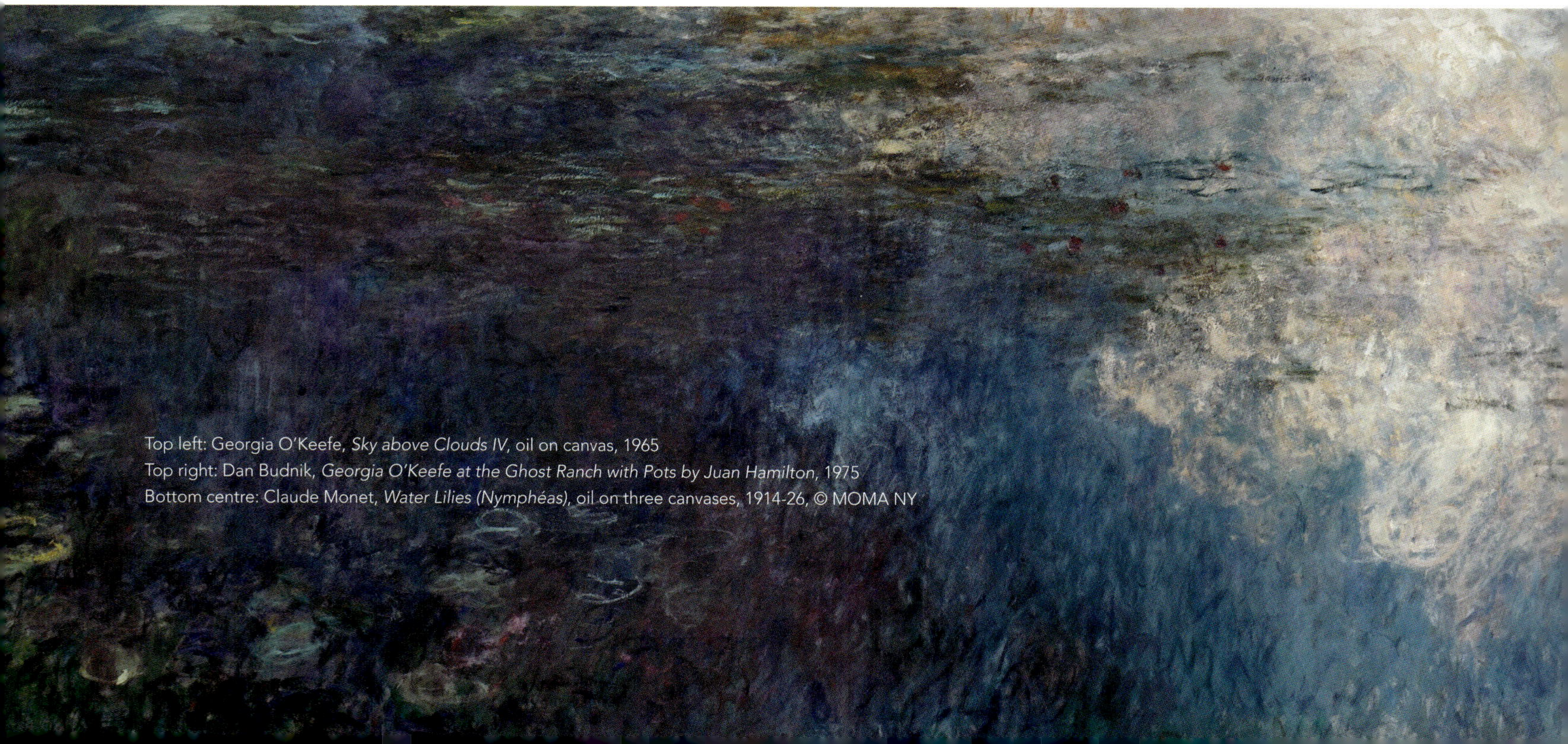

Top left: Georgia O'Keefe, *Sky above Clouds IV*, oil on canvas, 1965
Top right: Dan Budnik, *Georgia O'Keefe at the Ghost Ranch with Pots by Juan Hamilton*, 1975
Bottom centre: Claude Monet, *Water Lilies (Nymphéas)*, oil on three canvases, 1914-26, © MOMA NY

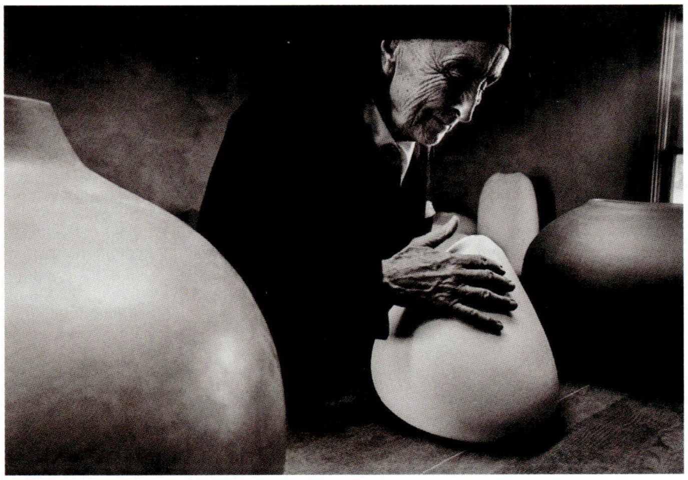

same thinking that sees blurriness, elongation, or distortion in painting as an error to be corrected. How much easier to presume that an artist has strayed from reality by mistake, or through illness, and not with intention or from some unutterable instinct. There's a persuasive romance, too, in this image of the stricken artist fighting against his errant nature. Witness the litany of diagnoses – from epilepsy to lead poisoning, syphilis to schizophrenia and bipolarity – that some suggest account for the intensity of Van Gogh's last paintings.

Look now at the Musée d'Orsay photograph: there is the familiar, paternal Monet of the public imagination. Read Dr Ravin's account, and you discover the ill-tempered, impatient, apprehensive and recurrently depressed individual who hid behind that image. But look at the water lily paintings themselves: there is a profound energy, a potent and raging energy in these paintings that are normally held up as icons of tranquillity, Monet grasping for a vitality he felt was, quite literally, fading from sight. The water garden at Giverny, a cloistered world of privacy, is thrown open. The elements are embraced: a painting of a pond becomes a mirror to the sky, its wet and shimmery surface effected in an arid expanse of scrapes and stains – very close, in fact, to the surface of Gérard's pots before the fire gives them their sheen – its peculiar, recessive focus threatening to tip us headfirst into the water. Is it too much to imagine Monet, struggling to discern between one colour and another on his palette, leaning instead into the physicality of paint, feeling his way into it, the strokes and tendrils and swirls that describe not the serene water above and the floating pads, but the eddies underneath, the movement of fish and frogs and insects buzzing over its surface, the whistling, chirruping, and bubbling noise of the garden, stems and shoots troubling the black water in the wind.

Monet called these late masterpieces, permanently installed after his death in the Musée de l'Orangerie, his *grandes décorations*. He meant by the term the professional definition of large works intended for a particular architectural setting, and often without a well-defined narrative. O'Keefe, who described her 24-foot cloud painting as 'ridiculous' but could not resist its impressive scale, might have given hers the same name. Certainly it describes the large vases and platters of Jean-Nicolas Gérard too: a magnanimous and embracing vision, not just of colour and light but in feeling, tactile, sensuous, rich to every perceptive faculty. In works like these there will always be more than meets the eye.

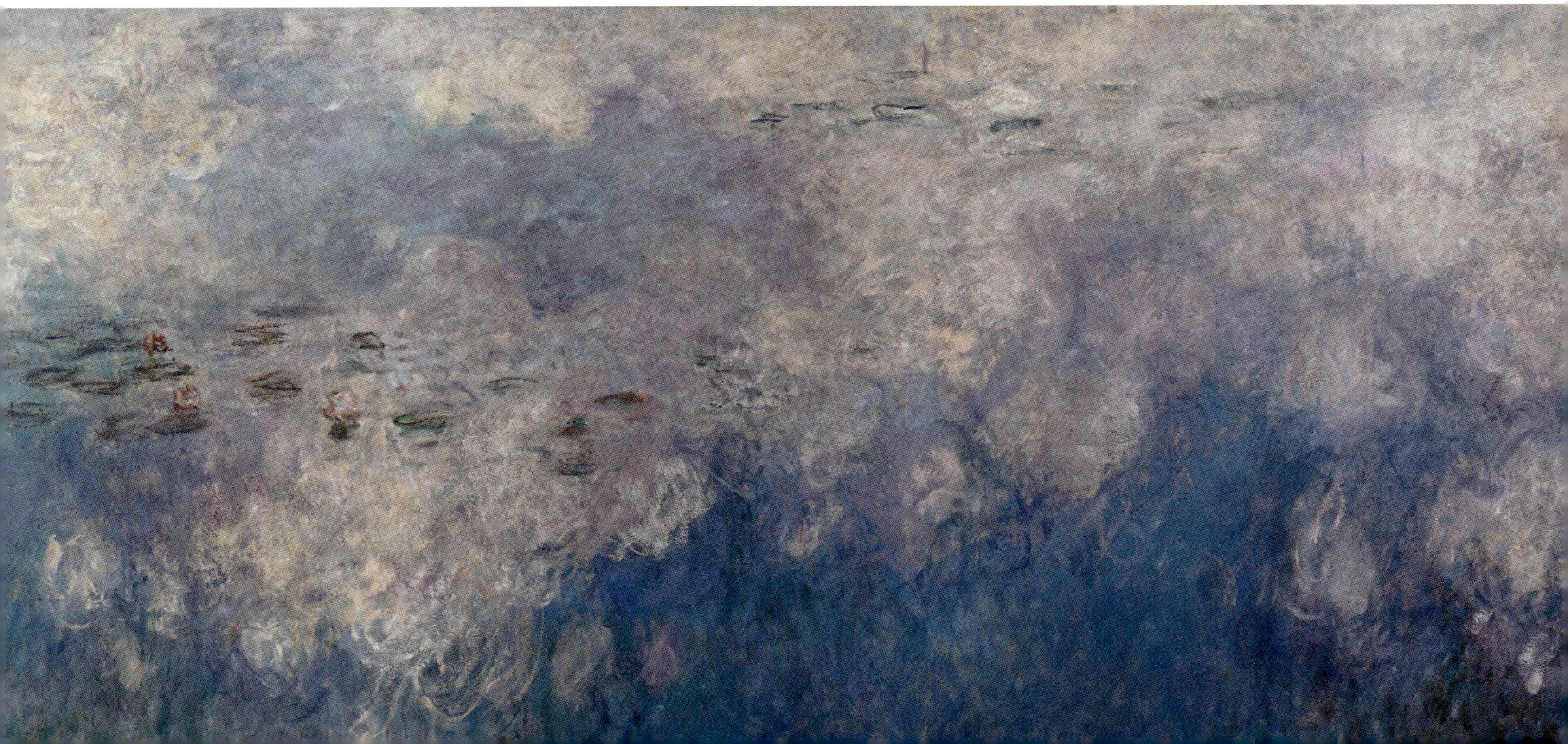

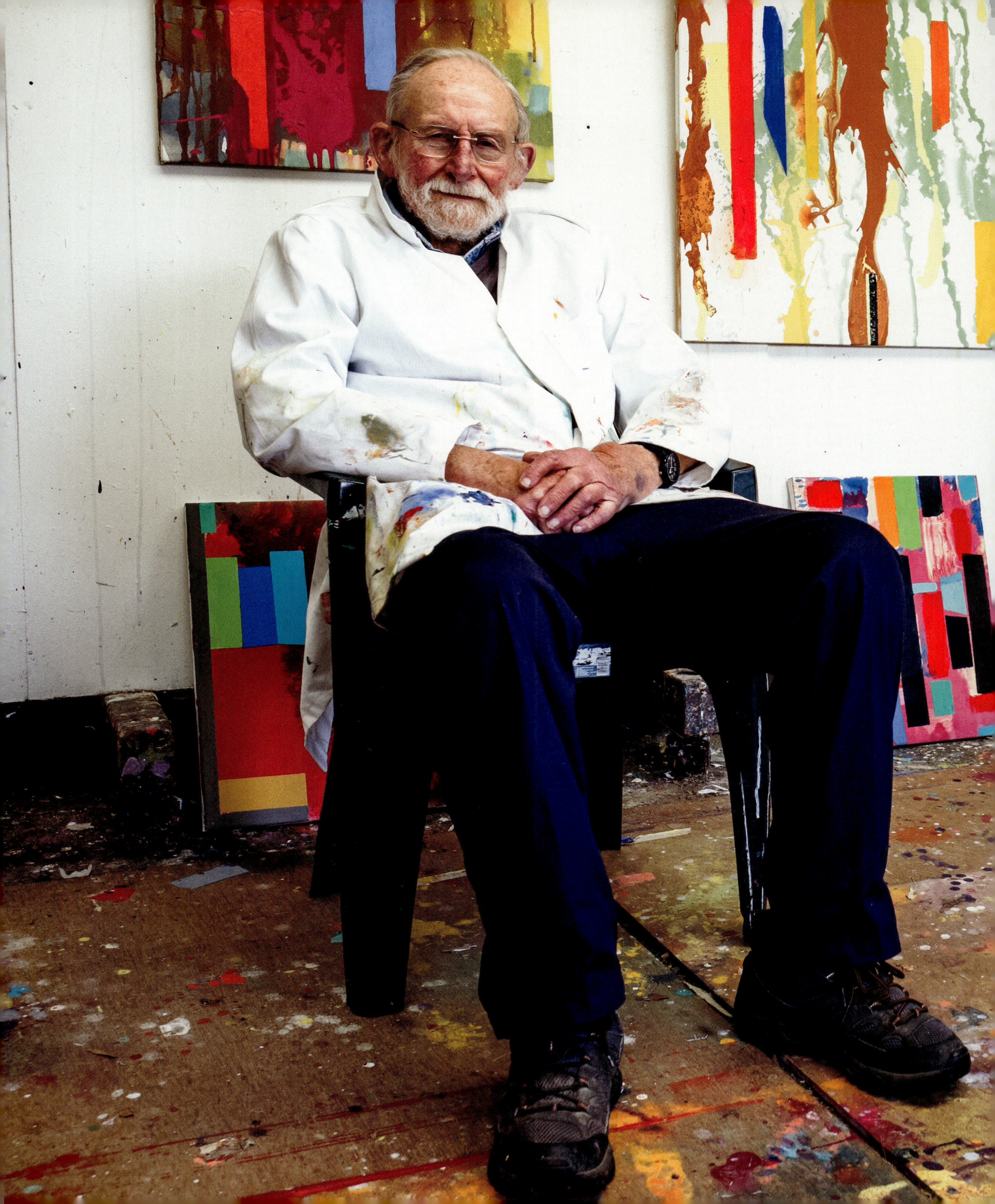

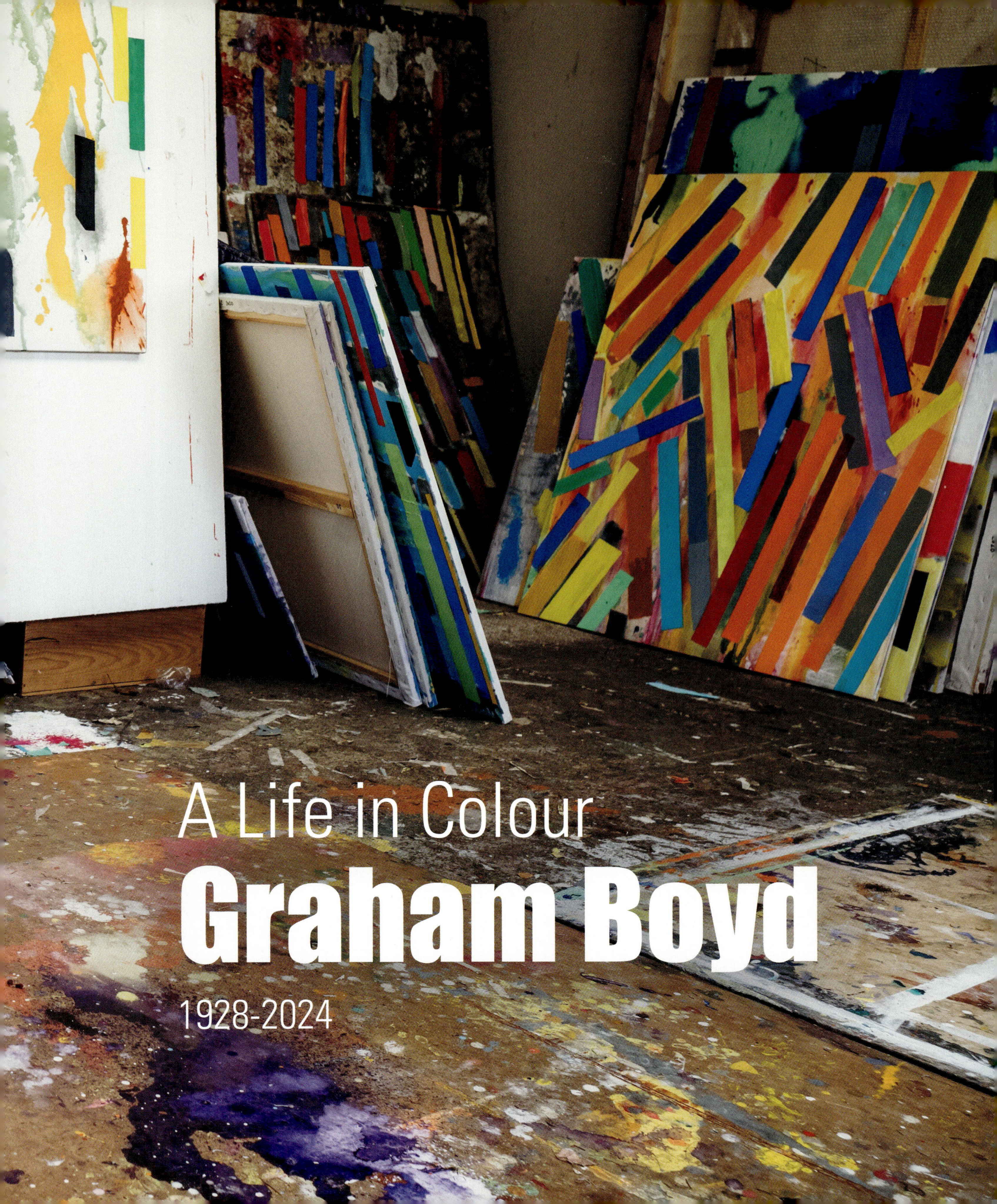

A Life in Colour

Graham Boyd

1928-2024

We were deeply saddened to hear that Graham Boyd had passed away earlier this summer, just weeks ahead of his second Goldmark show.

This interview, recorded in his studio two years ago, reveals the enthusiasm he had for his art, undiminished to the end.

Graham, we are sitting in your sun-lit studio in Chipperfield, Hertfordshire, surrounded by every possible colour of paint you could imagine. Would you say these two things, light and colour, are the foundation of your work?

Yes, well, light is the thing. When you think about it, when you paint you're working with colour, but you're trying to convey a sense of light. And light, according to Newton, comprises the colours of the spectrum. Mix all the colours of the rainbow and you get white light; but mix all the colours of the paint box and you get black. That's called subtractive mixing. And it's the great paradox of painting that the painter tries to create white light out of black light – like the alchemist trying to make gold out of lead. It's one of the reasons why painting is such a marvellous activity. And that is to say nothing of the psychological side of colour. Imagine you're cold and you see a fire: the heat of the flames is very welcoming, but fire can be threatening too, can't it? I recall reading that Kandinsky would test his students on what colour generates which emotion. Red for him was terrestrial, it was solid, it

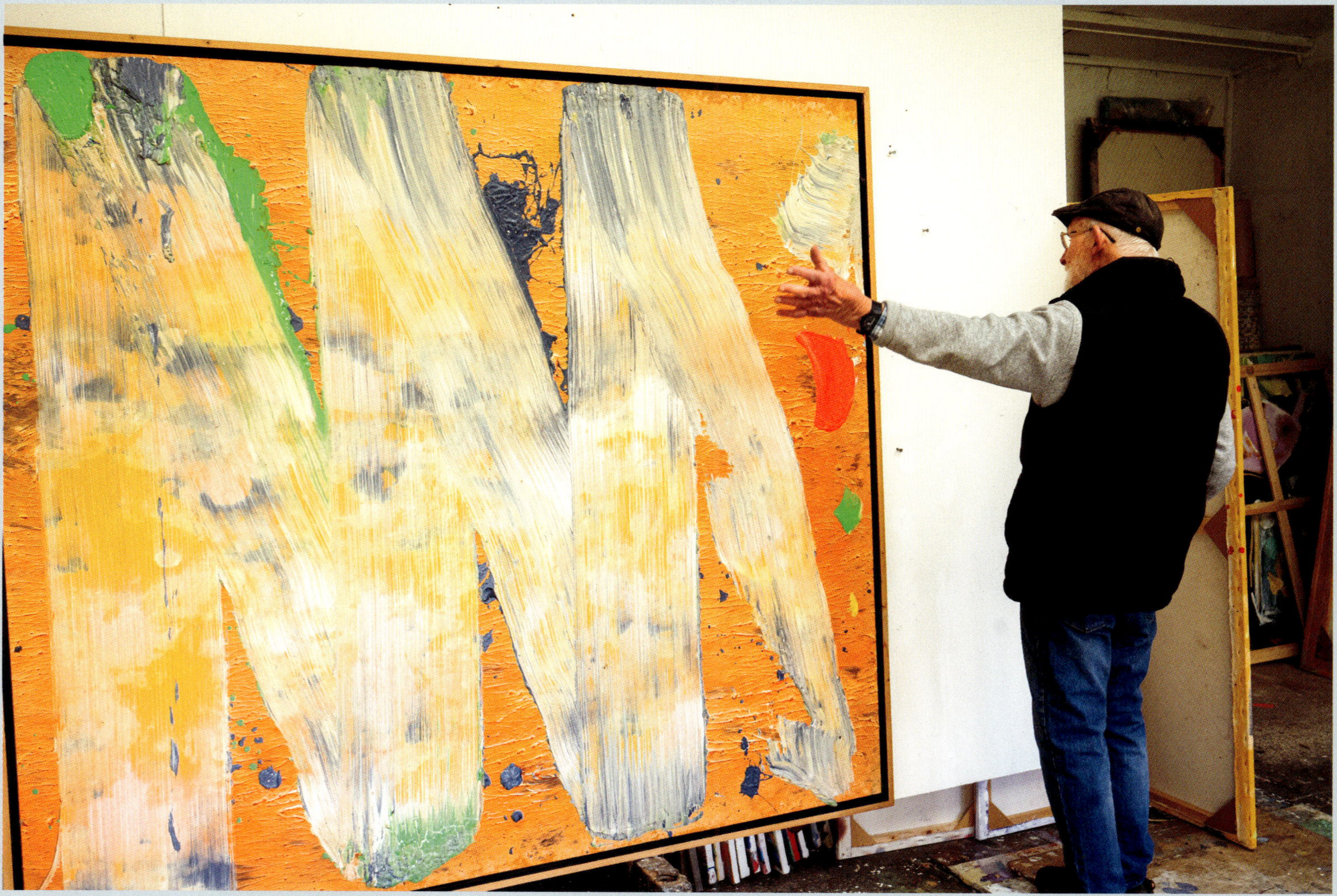

was earth, the Egyptian symbol of a field. Yellow was rapacious, was aggressive, but it's also the light of the sun. All these colours have a duality. Blue gives you that feeling of heaven, peace, tranquillity, but it can also make you feel cold. Colours have their opposite poles, and I think that's why it's such a fascinating language. Even when you just use it as spoken language, it evokes those feelings, doesn't it? But to actually see it – to see a certain red and green creating a harmony, like a musical chord. Red against green gives you a particular sonority.

You didn't actually start as a painter, did you, let alone an abstract one? Take us back to the beginning of your career.

No, I didn't. I was born in Bristol in 1928 – just a couple of years after the death of Claude Monet, to throw out a hook to art history, and right between two world wars. My father served in both of them: as a boy in the trenches, just 18 years old, and then again in the RAF in the 1940s, right through the war. I was lucky that the war was over by the time I was 18. I just had to do things like guard duty, and I was stationed in North Africa for that, in Tripoli for a short while. When I came back to art school I did book illustration. I always found I had a little bit of a flair for it. I remember seeing a copy of Oliver Twist in Watford Public Library when I was about 13, I suppose, with these etched illustrations by George Cruikshank. There was that famous picture of Fagan in the condemned cell, biting his nails. I was just fascinated. I had to read whole chunks of Dickens to get to an explanation of that illustration. But I loved Cruikshank and I tried to emulate him in my efforts.

It was very hard to get work as an illustrator after I graduated. I did the rounds with my portfolio. I was working up in the fens in a secondary school as an art teacher, living in a tiny room where I soon found myself painting rather than illustrating. More and more often there would be a painting on an easel in the bedroom where I slept, breathing deeply the turpentine fumes and white spirit at night, but waking up and seeing what I had on the easel. Far more exciting than a piece of paper in a portfolio, and it was that interesting structure that grew and grew with me.

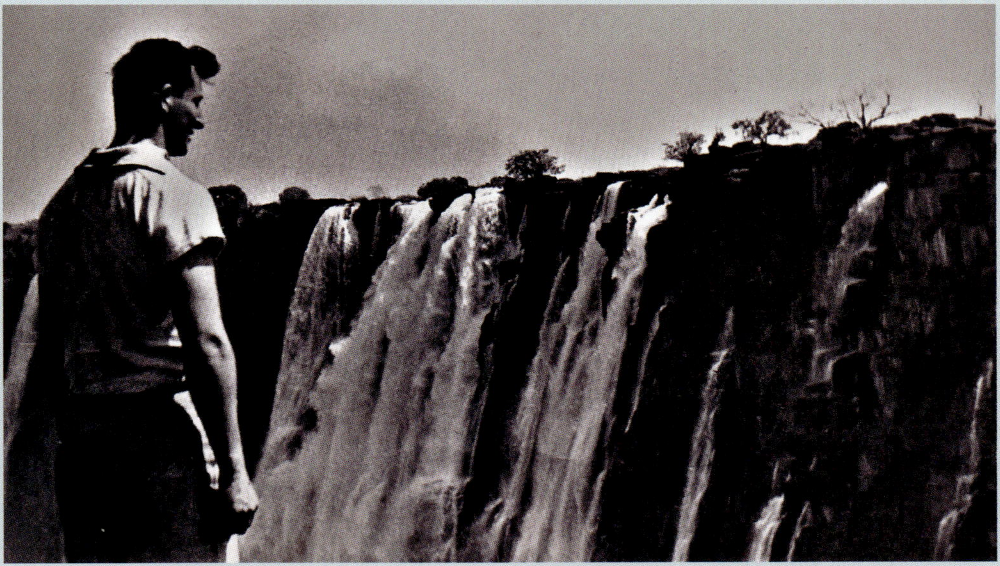

Tell me how you came to be living and working in Africa.

When I was a student I had met a girl, a tobacco farmer's daughter in what was then Southern Rhodesia (now Zimbabwe). We became engaged and I eventually went to meet her family.

England in that drab, post-war period of the early '50s, everything was run down, the people were run down. Then to go to a place where the sun shone and it was expansive. Out in Rhodesia I made paintings that were based on landscape, but it was an art of the imagination which appealed to me rather than one based on strict observation. That was the change within me, when I was in Rhodesia. While I was out there I met the ceramicist Professor William Staite Murray and he became a kind of mentor to me, because he'd been a painter before he became a potter. His influence stayed with me, and also his embrace of Buddhism, and that oriental idea of space being active, rather in the way we think of it in atomic theory.

When I returned to England, I began to reflect on the African experience. I thought of it as something that was made out of myriads of energy points, like atoms, electrons, particles. You see flocks of birds, termites, you know, mass movement of things and creatures, grains of sand even. There is that William Blake line about a grain of sand and the whole of eternity. I particularly was drawn to the idea of chance as being a way of achieving breakthroughs, of taking risks, and I learnt that you had to take risks. You couldn't just go on producing work in a single, straight chronology, a kind of pedantic process. You had sometimes to be able to rise to impulse and to leaps of the imagination. That's something I still hold dear, has become part of my attitude and approach. But as time went by, my paintings began to veer more towards the third dimension.

Opposite: *Advance*, acrylic on canvas, 1992
Above: Overlooking Victoria Falls, 1954

'Some people classify them as the Apollonian, the more rational operation of the human brain, and the Dionysian, which is instinctive, the wild side. And sometimes I go one way, sometimes the other…'

Had you begun to paint abstractly then?

No, not really. I came back to England – the relationship with the tobacco farmer's daughter was a terrible disaster in the end. When I returned, I was still working figuratively for a year or two. But gradually I became more and more interested in not just that English tradition of poetic illustration, artists like Paul Nash and Graham Sutherland – like me, they had both been quite graphic artists in their early days, but in French painting especially. In Rhodesia I had started to look at Impressionism, at Cezanne, Degas, Gauguin, and then of course Picasso and Braque and Matisse. I was aware of modern art, but there was very little going on in London. It all felt very parochial.

Fear is a thing in England. When I was growing up, there was a fear of colour. I don't think it's like that now, but for a long time, because we lived in a foggier climate in the old days – I remember the pea-soupers. Monet came to London for the fogs. But it's that hesitancy about colour, toning things down all the time, which I wanted to break out of.

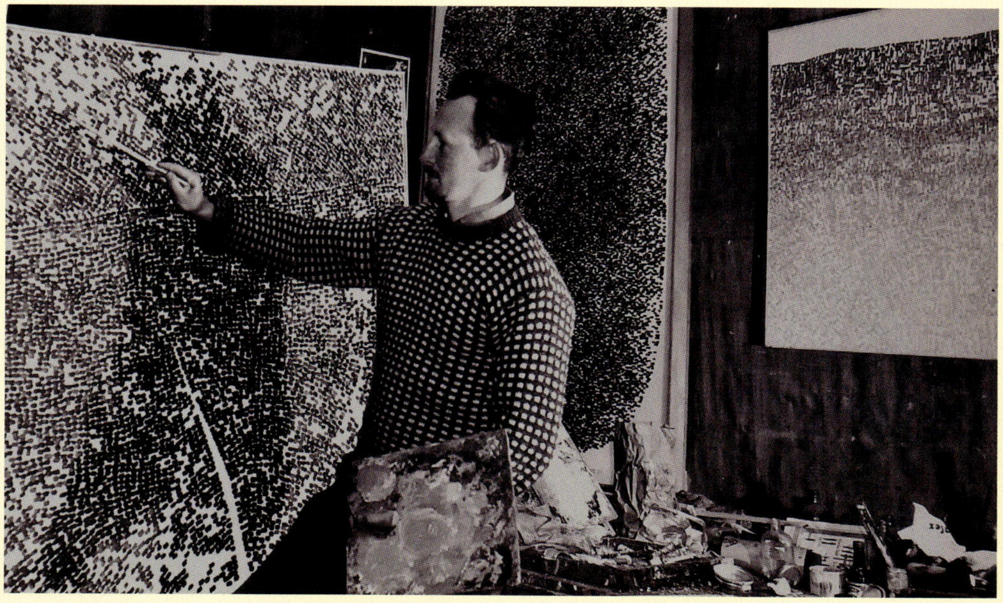

What was the catalyst for that breakthrough?

Well there were many, but I discovered the works of Hans Hoffmann. He had led a revolt amongst the younger generation against the more nationalist American painters who wanted to paint folksy scenes of the American rural west, very much out of touch of with what had been happening in Europe. But there were a lot of young American painters who were in the habit of going to Paris to study, and in the end, thanks to people like Hoffmann and others, there was a breakthrough, largely during the war years, of people like Jackson Pollock, who'd worked with Hoffmann, Mark Rothko, Barnett Newman and others, where something big and powerful started to happen in the work. I became more aware of the roots of this development. I began to read Mondrian's theories – managed to find this one little book with his essays in it. Mondrian had made this classic shift from paintings of buildings where he looked more at the verticals and horizontals of facades, or looking at the branches in apple trees and the spaces between the branches. Each version he painted had become more and more abstract. I kind of latched onto that and that became my language.

An abstraction from nature?

More the fact that one had to be quite radical in one's thinking, you know, he had to be a bit of a Calvinist. I remember as a child reading about the Civil War, the roundheads and the cavaliers, I was fascinated by Oliver Cromwell. I liked the fact that the Cromwellians were very strict and didn't dress in a fancy way like the cavaliers, and had God on their side! I was quite religious in those days. Mondrian wouldn't use a diagonal even. He only believed in verticals and horizontals. That Calvinist side, I have that

price guide inside back cover

in my nature, but at the same time I have the opposite side. Some people classify them as the Apollonian, the more rational operation of the human brain, and the Dionysian, which is instinctive, the wild side. And sometimes I go one way, sometimes the other. Painting is all about opposites – of colour, tone, texture, scale – and reconciling the two somehow.

To begin with, I wasn't thinking so much that I was making abstract or semi-abstract paintings. I began by painting skies but leaving out the land. With clouds, you've got things shifting around all the time. And then I noticed structures forming. In my front room above the fireplace there's a painting from a memory in Rhodesia of the way the rains came in the autumn, and they would fall like tails coming down out of the clouds. I began to think of everything as being made out of fibres, like a muscle or a tree, if you like: it's got a plank grain and it's got an end grain. Cut it one way and you've got lines, cut it the other way and you've got dots.

I can see that in the sculptures you made very clearly – the boxes and structures made from nylon thread, Perspex, plastic beads. How did that idea translate in your drawing and painting?

I became fascinated with the use of a grid. There are drawings I've got, from around 1974-5 in America when I didn't have a studio, in which the work is very controlled, performed with a rapidograph pen and a straight edge, all investigating grids as a way of exploring space as something granular, atomic, something which is in everything and everywhere. That idea of particles being the basis – I was trying to think of space in that way, that it had a structure to it and you could invent different structures as you saw fit.

I was also very aware of the relationship of painting to music, to sound. You know

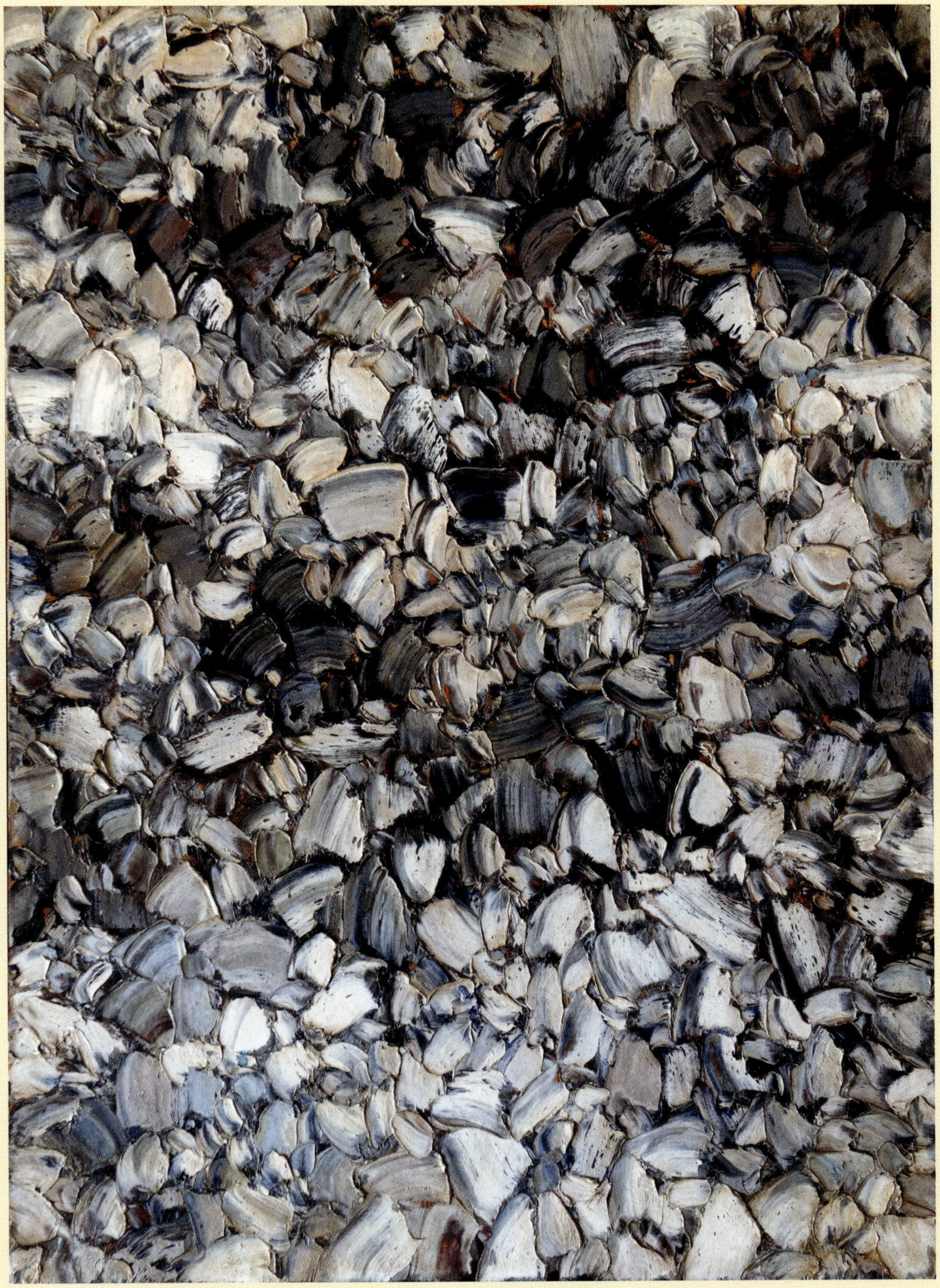

Opposite: Meadow Studios, Bushey, 1962
Above: *Lost Gully*, oil on canvas, 1969

when you hear church bells pealing, I wanted to make paintings that pealed in a way, using verticals packed together. Each one sits in space and corresponds to another, and they sort of 'sound off' each other, a visual equivalence of sound. Some of these I finished just a few years ago, but they're sitting on this grid-like structure that has been buried since 1972. Early on I think I was trying to lose some of that autobiographical quality in the painting, but that incredible precision that the grid offers has actually liberated some of the freer interpretation that I'm doing now, they seem to go together. Someone said that greatness of ideas is precision of ideas. So for me the grid is just completely endless in its possibilities.

Where were you painting when you came back from Africa?

I got a place in Bushey at Meadow Studios – a series of rooms built by Sir Hubert von Herkomer R.A. in the 1890s, for his followers and former students. And this was of major importance, because it gave me that sense of how vital it was to have space, to not try and work in a tiny, cramped up way. The roof leaked terribly, but when you walked into that space the light was magic, like being in a cathedral. Ralph Rumney and the New Yorker Robert Moscowitz worked in nearby studios, as did Gwyther Irwin, who was making a name for himself at that time. He was well connected with people like Lawrence

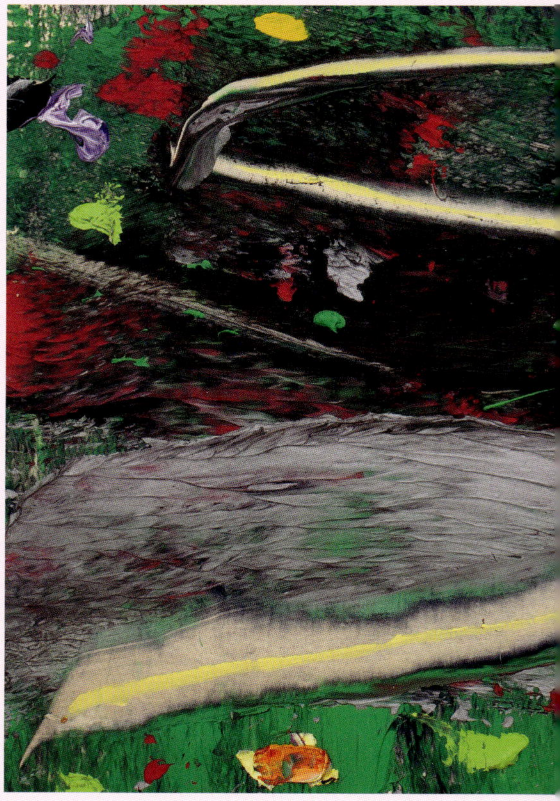

Below: *Hector*, acrylic on canvas, 2017
Opposite top: *Turismo Rurale*, acrylic on canvas, 1995
Opposite bottom: *New Hampshire Grid*, etching, 1974

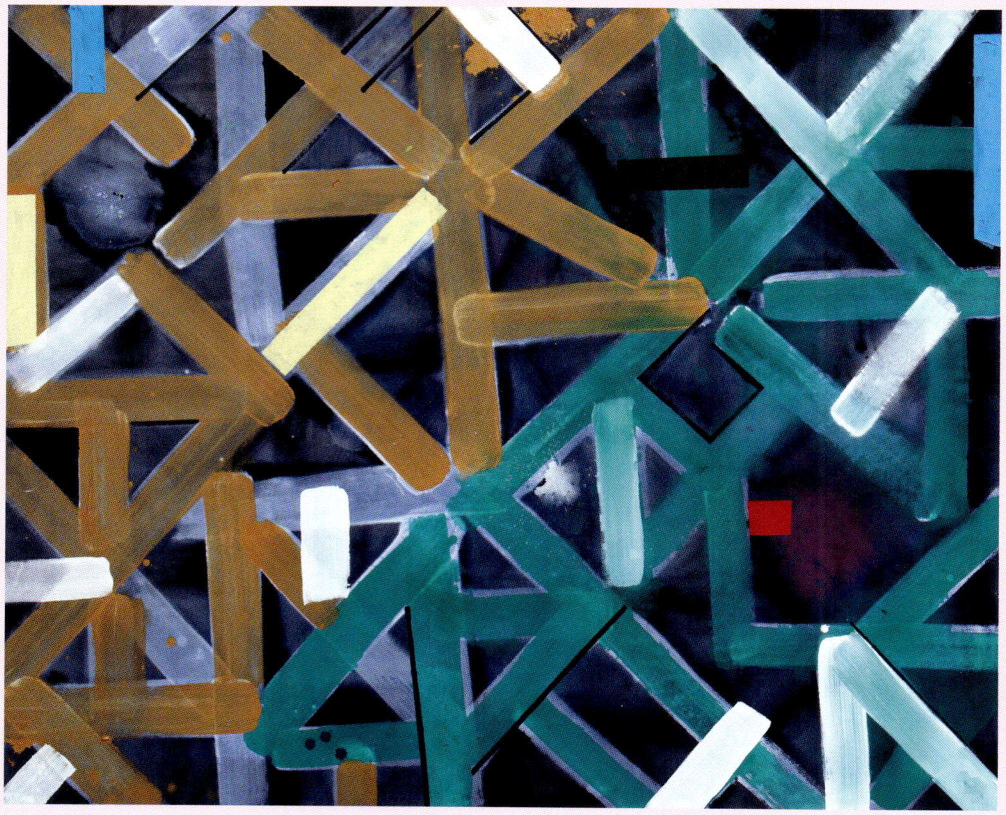

Alloway, Dick Smith, that whole generation of people at the Royal College who suddenly emerged in that Pop Art era. They would come down to the Meadows and fall in the fire and get drunk and have pretty wild parties. It was so different from the life, only four or five miles away, that my parents were living in a semi-detached on the edge of Cassiobury Park. When I went down to stay with them, I felt I would suffocate, you know. I was out in a different world.

And then you came to America for the first time – another very different world!

Yes. I had married then; we went to America with our two children. I'd been given the chance of a teaching exchange in New Hampshire, which turned out to be a huge adventure. A challenge, too. We moved from one place to another,

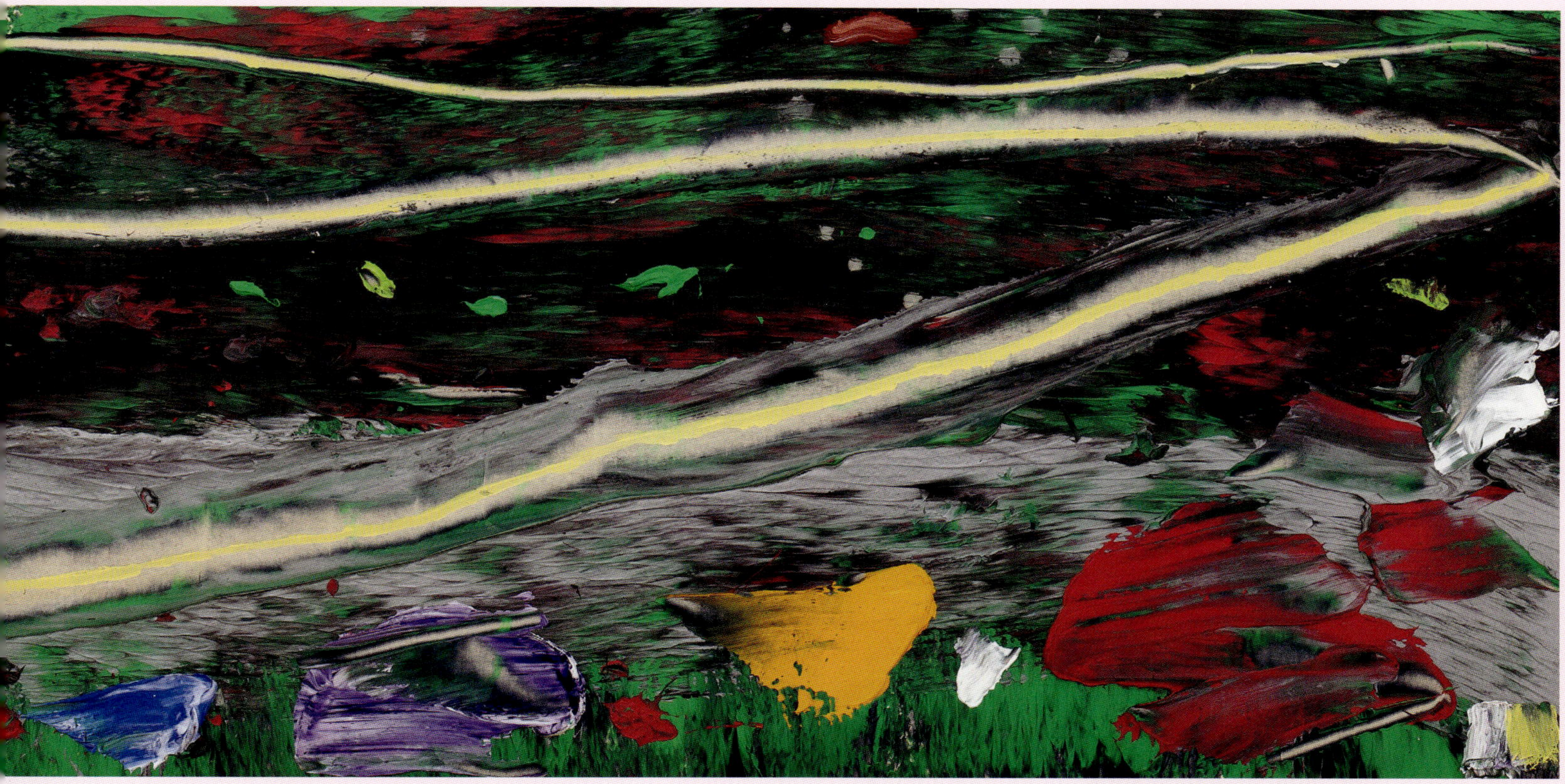

living in American society, which seemed tremendously friendly and generous. But it was the year of the energy crisis – Nixon's being kicked out and you weren't allowed to drive more than 55 miles an hour to save energy. We had this little Volkswagen and we decided to visit some friends we had in Colorado. We drove what must have been nearly 2,000 miles west, the kids lying horizontally on the back seat as we chuntered along, taking it in turns to do the driving. Eventually we ran out of new tarmac highway, onto less firm looking roads – at one point we even ran into a tornado. Then the extraordinary climax of reaching the Grand Canyon. There are certain moments, huge moments, that have happened to me in my life which have given me the kind of basis for my work, my sensibility, dare I say, most of them to do with landscape. Though I'm an abstract painter, if there is

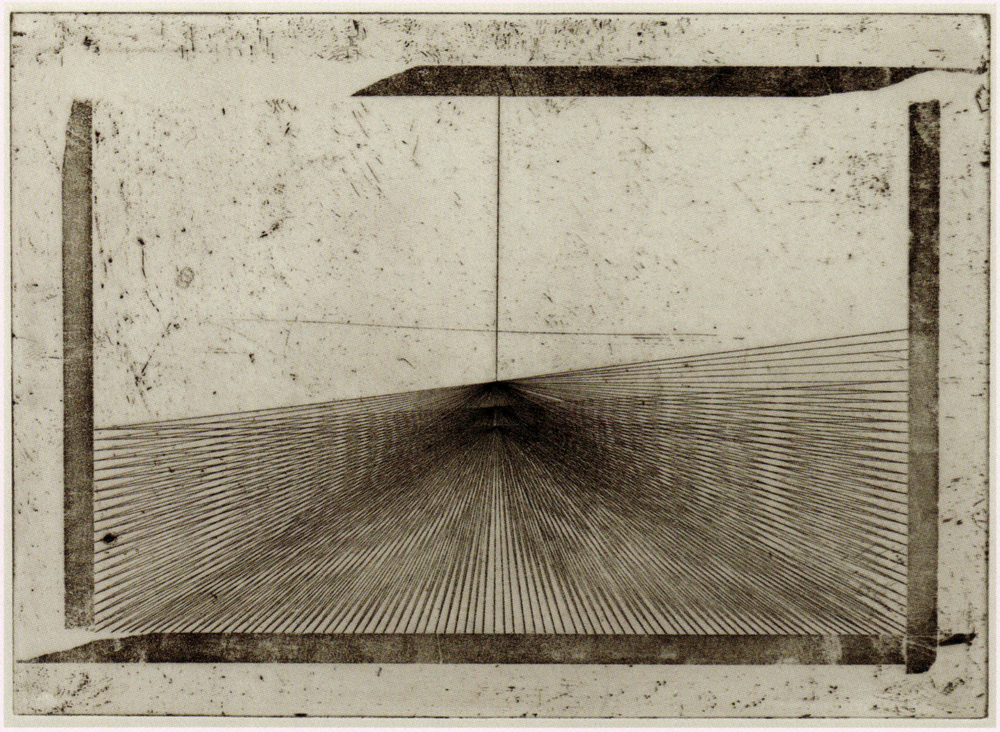

such a thing – what is abstraction anyway? It's got to be about something – the things that move me, more than anything else, are landscapes, and that tremendous sense of scale. Big countries, big horizons.

Do you miss that sense of scale here in the UK?

Well I don't feel it's been a proper day until I've had a walk. There's a lane from here to the entrance to the woods – about half a mile. I vary the route every day. And it's something that gives me pleasure really. It's physical exercise, but one sees things – round, flat, rough, smooth, cause and effect. How trees fall and time passes and the drama of the actual event gets moved over. That sort of thing's going on in painting all the time. You introduce a colour and it has an effect on those around it. Decay is fascinating to see. Years ago, they used to come logging down here and we would walk over the ruts that the carts had left. More recently, children have been making trails with their bicycles, making tracks. In time, nature will take over again. And that sort of constant flux between the activity of man and the activity of nature will continue, I suppose, until they cut the woods down, heaven forbid.

You went back to America again, later?

I'd been working at the Hertfordshire College of Art and Design for some time – perhaps seven or eight years – when I heard about the Triangle Workshop, which had already been running for one year. Anthony Caro had set it up, and it was an international workshop held in Upstate New York, with artists coming largely from the UK, Canada and the United States. I applied for it and was accepted. I think John Hoyland was invited – Larry Poons attended, and Tony Caro was very friendly with Clement Greenberg, who offered critiques along with Helen Frankenthaler, people like that. It was almost like being a student again. We each had an 8 foot by 8 foot painting deck and people would pass by,

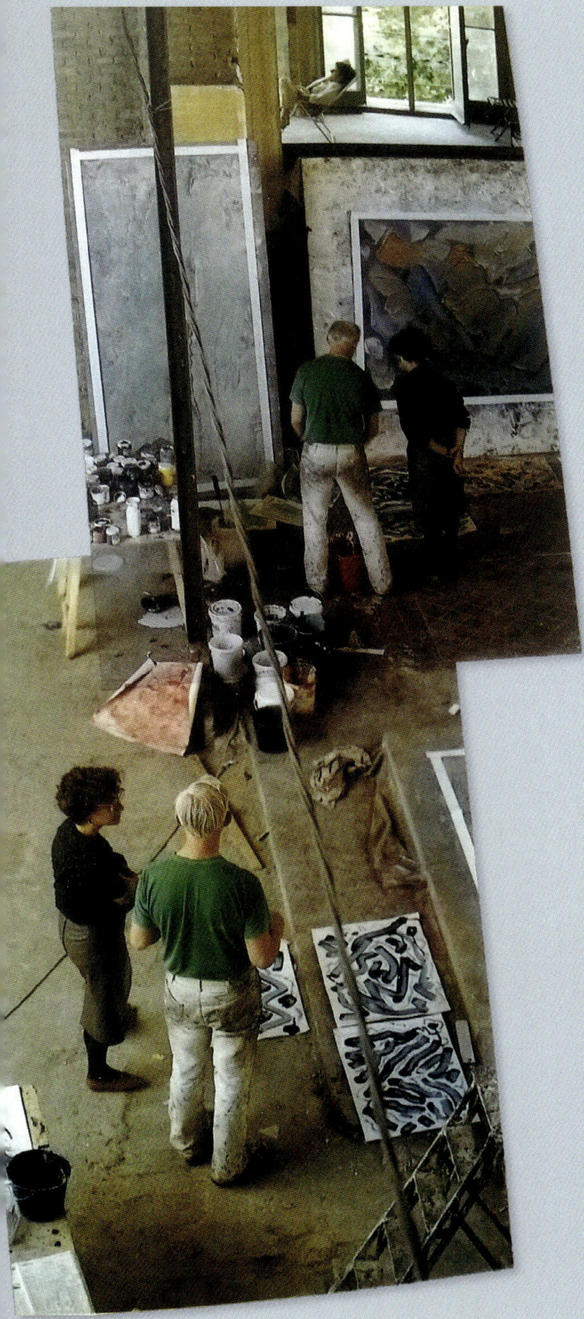

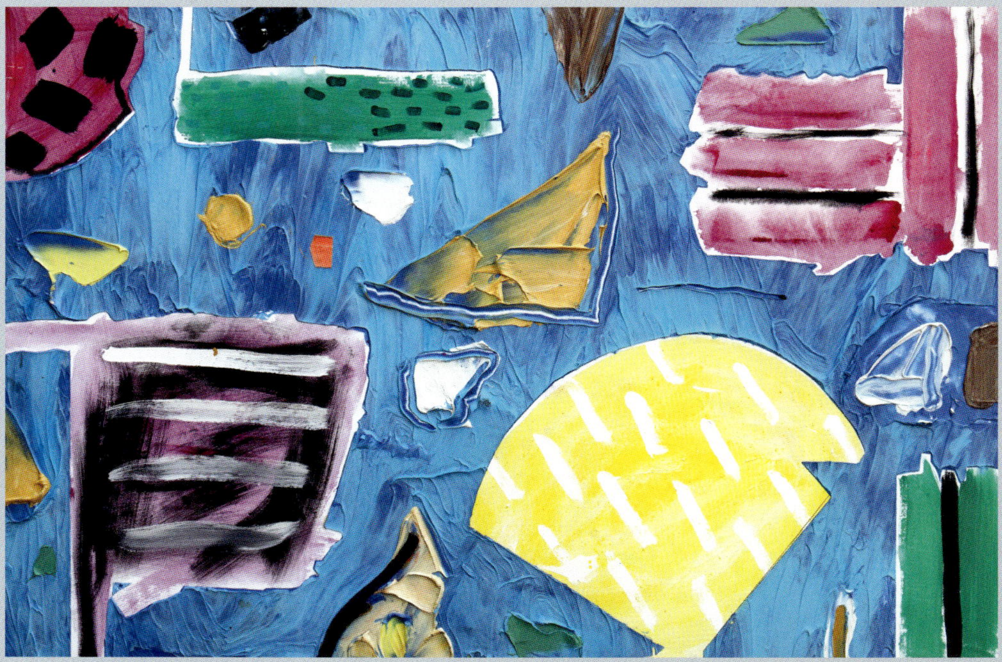

Above: Critique with Theresa Blanche at the 1987 Triangle Workshop, Barcelona
Right: *Sat Nav*, acrylic on canvas, 2011
Opposite: *Laguna*, acrylic on canvas, 2002

giving opinions, offering helpful advice. It turned out everyone was very positive. There was no bitchiness, no jealousy. Everyone was trying to help everyone make good art. Out there I was doing maybe three big-ish paintings a day, because we were working fast. You were turning on your instinct rather than your intellect. You just went ahead and did it, whatever prompted you. That was the big difference really. It expanded my contacts, but it also expanded my own way of working. There is a terrific energy in America. There's no doubt about it.

After the workshop was over, I had an opportunity to get to know Anthony Caro and his wife Sheila, who was also an artist – extremely generous people. He bought some of my work and was very encouraging. He said of me that "I had the least ego of any artist in you." I don't know if it was a compliment or not really! But he would come and visit the students at St. Alban's where I was teaching and was very complimentary to the course we were running there. It's about generosity really. Here he was sharing himself in a way that major artists rarely do. And I learned quite a lot from him.

Did you adapt things from the workshop?

I have my own painting deck here now, and I often work on board then stretch the canvas later. At Triangle there was a tradition of cropping – something Bonnard had done too. I don't crop as much now, but it gives me some flexibility with what I'm doing.

I'll use strips of coloured paper as tryouts, like collage, later on in the painting, which sometimes helps me advance my decision-making. Where you put a colour or a form in a painting has an enormous impact: whether you opt for a rest zone, or a resonance, rather than just an easily anticipated accent. Practically any colour you put at the top of a

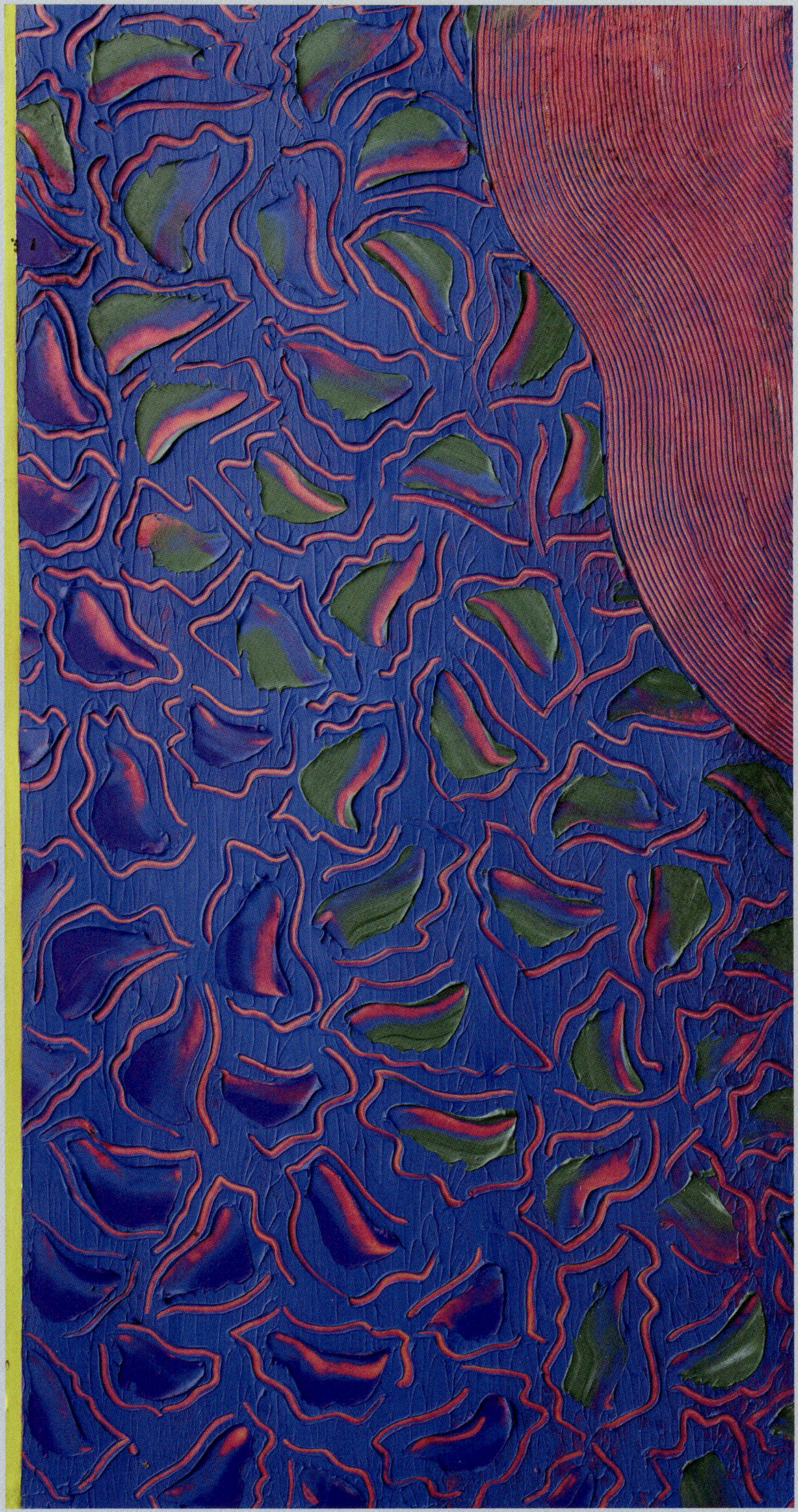

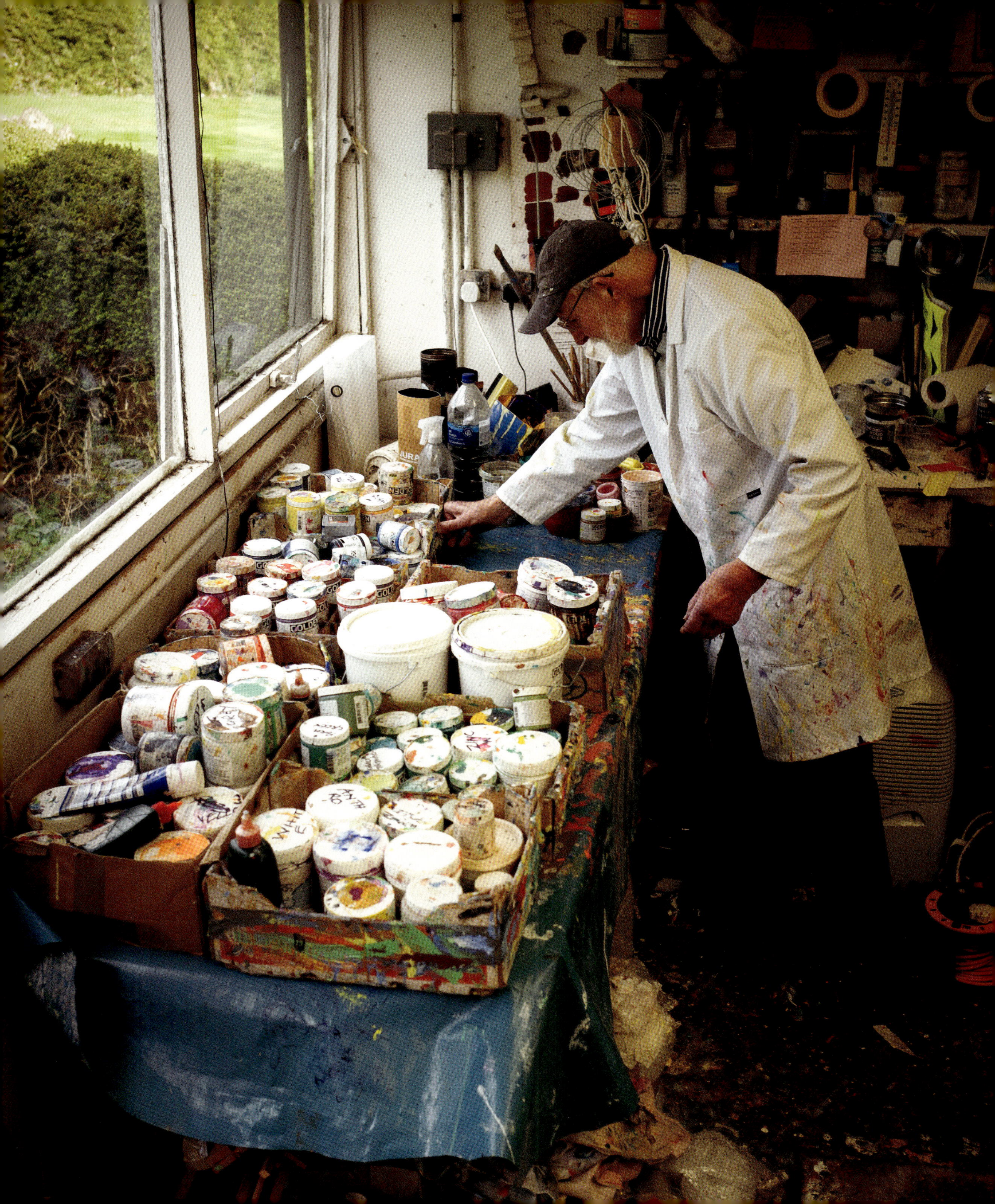
JURA

painting tries to recede, no matter how bright it is – that's quite interesting to cope with. But everything is about complementaries, I think. Everything's about contrast. While I'm painting, I'm thinking very much about things being in or out of focus, things being sharp, things being smooth.

I used to do a little bit of rock climbing and you sometimes have to go off balance a bit in order to make your move. Well likewise, you have to risk losing a good painting in order to get somewhere you haven't been before, to get out of your comfort zone. The idea of exploration – most of us have that kind of innate desire not to do the same old thing all the time. Very often those first marks have something special about them. Other times you've seen it all before. Or sometimes you get this idea that in order to achieve something, you sometimes have to break something. So sometimes the painting is going too well but it's too familiar. You know too much what the outcome is going to be and you have to be prepared to destroy that in order to get to the next stage – to put yourself off balance.

It was not that long ago that we were filming you for your first exhibition at the gallery. That film now has been viewed more than 160,000 times. Did that surprise you?

It's terribly exciting that the work has had such a reception; I'm very proud of that. I'm 94 years old now, and I've been painting since I was in my late 20s. Things have changed, but it's given me a chance to get a perspective on what I've been doing. I remember reading when Pollock was doing his pour work, he was saying to himself, "Am I a phony? Is this art?" I felt like that at times – when I was doing those 1960 palette knife paintings. I remember thinking, 'This isn't how people make paintings!' But when I look at them now, there's something organic about them that I believe was true and honest.

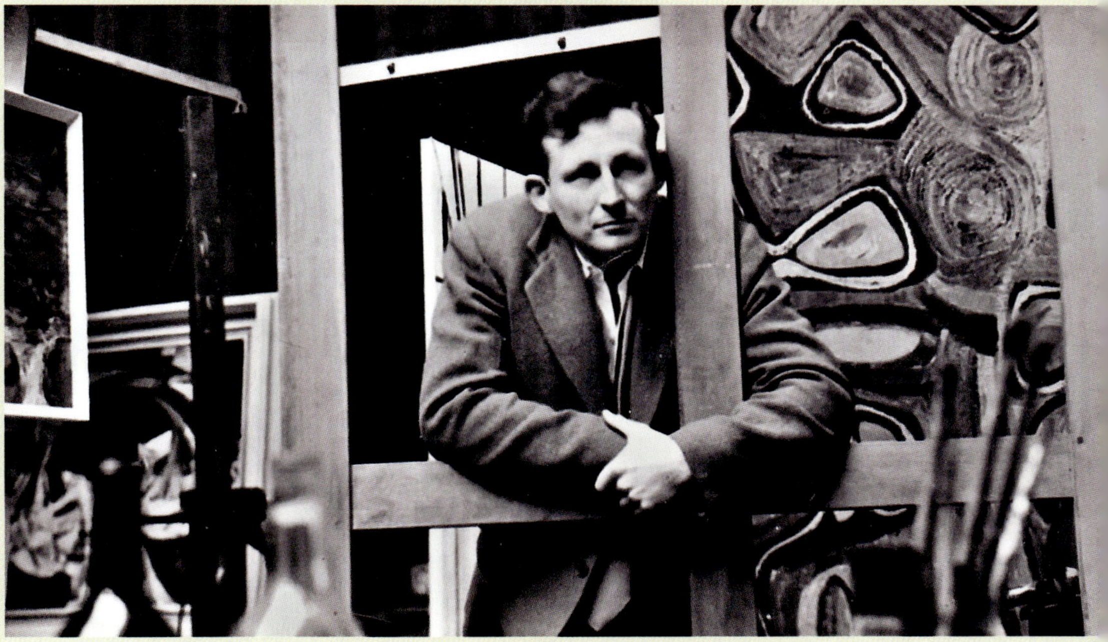

Above: Meadow Studios, Bushey, 1956
Below: *Alto*, acrylic on canvas, 2018

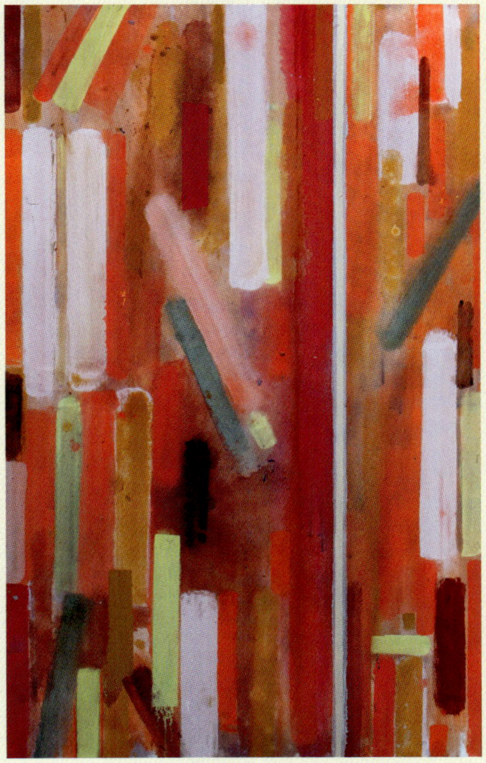

As I've got older, the enormity of painting as an area of activity has grown and grown. It's a way of knowing you're alive, that you paint. Painting, even now, gives me that freedom. I can do something on a blank canvas that no one's ever done before. That's a heck of a gift, isn't it, to be in that position?

I realise what a big art form it is, how all-encompassing it is. And I feel I don't always know what I'm doing. In fact, you know, there's quite a bit of that: you find the reason afterwards. But life's like that, isn't it? You never know what's going to happen tomorrow.

Graham Boyd had continued to paint daily in his studio in preparation for his upcoming 2024 exhibition at Goldmark.

This will still go ahead, now as a Memorial Show, opening October 26th.

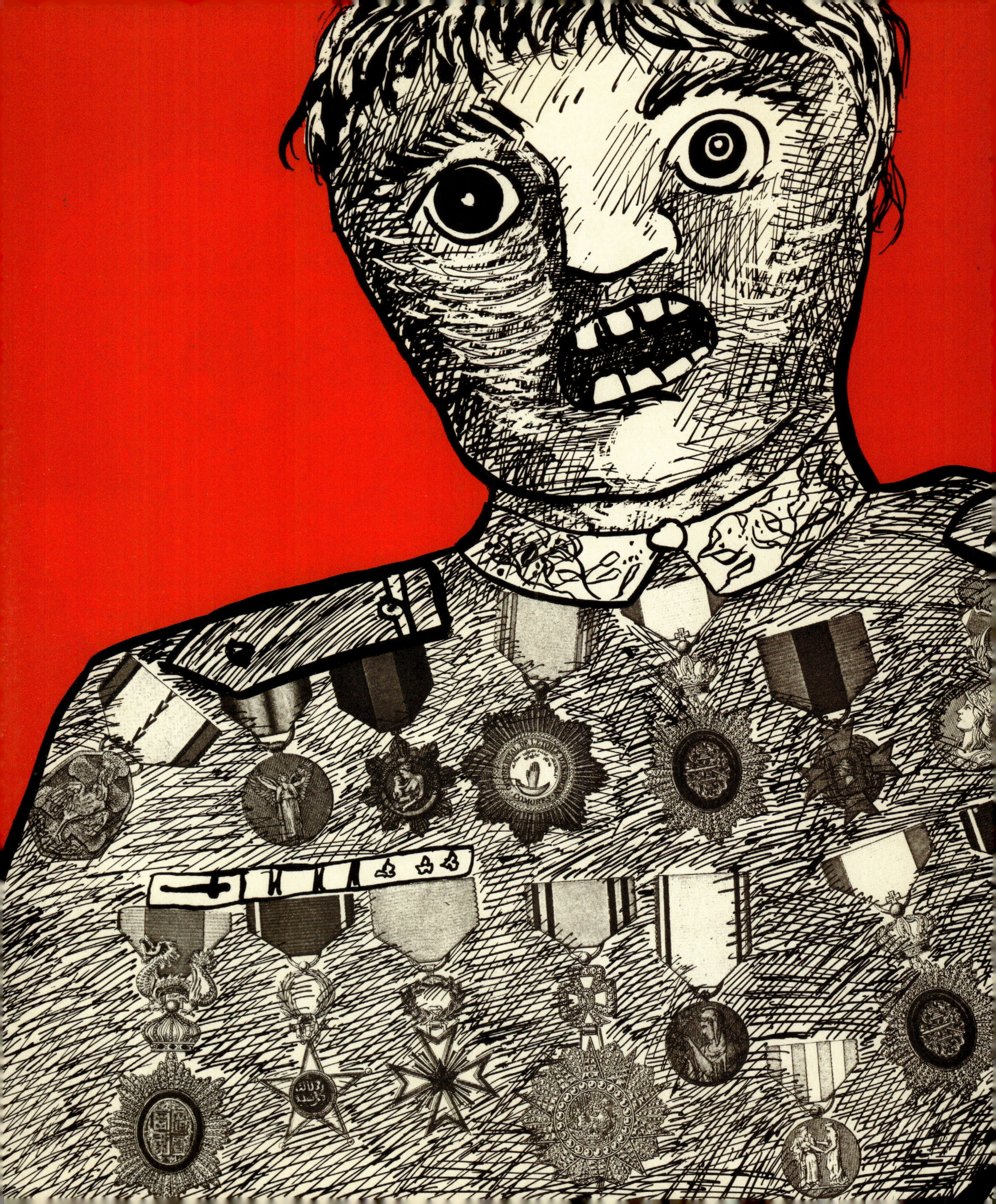

Enrico Baj

Enfant Terrible

From his hysterical Generals to his eccentric bricolage collages, the Italian 'Nuclear Artist' savaged political corruption with childlike abandon

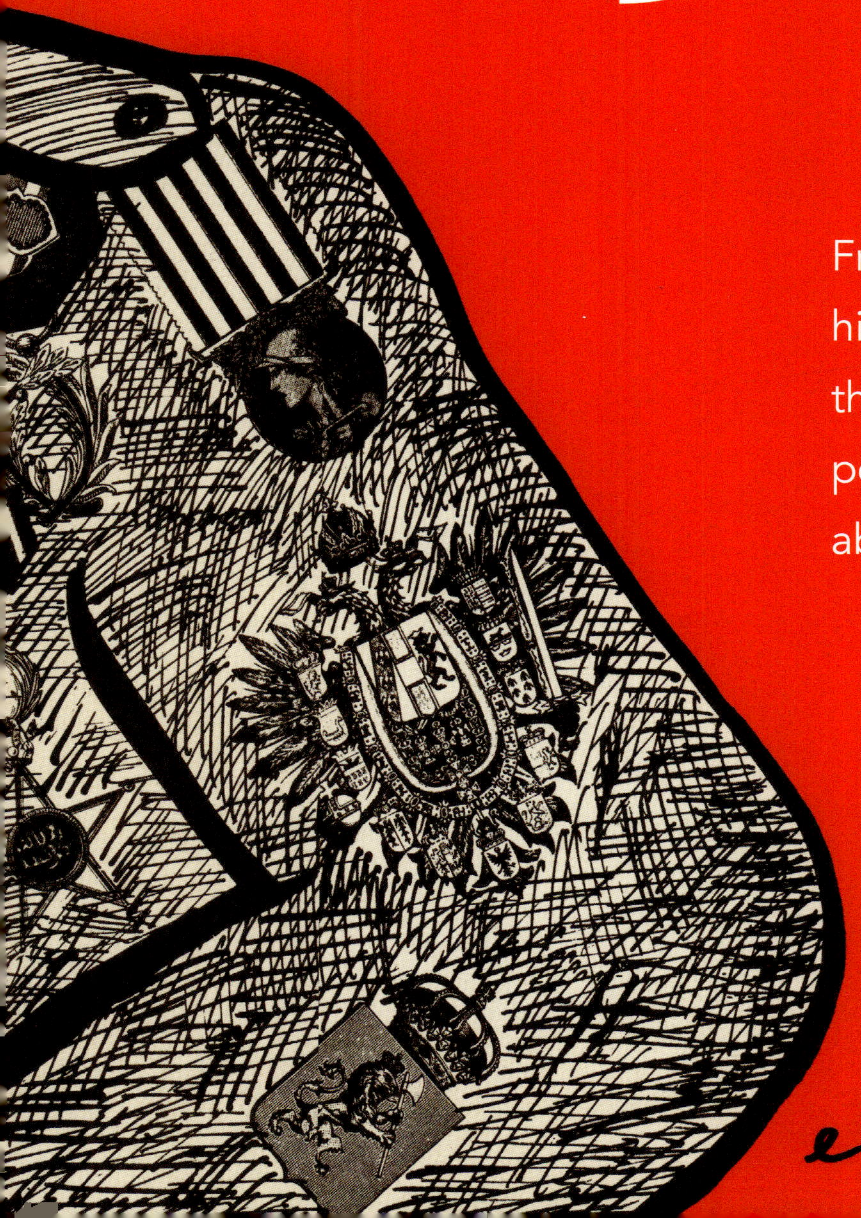

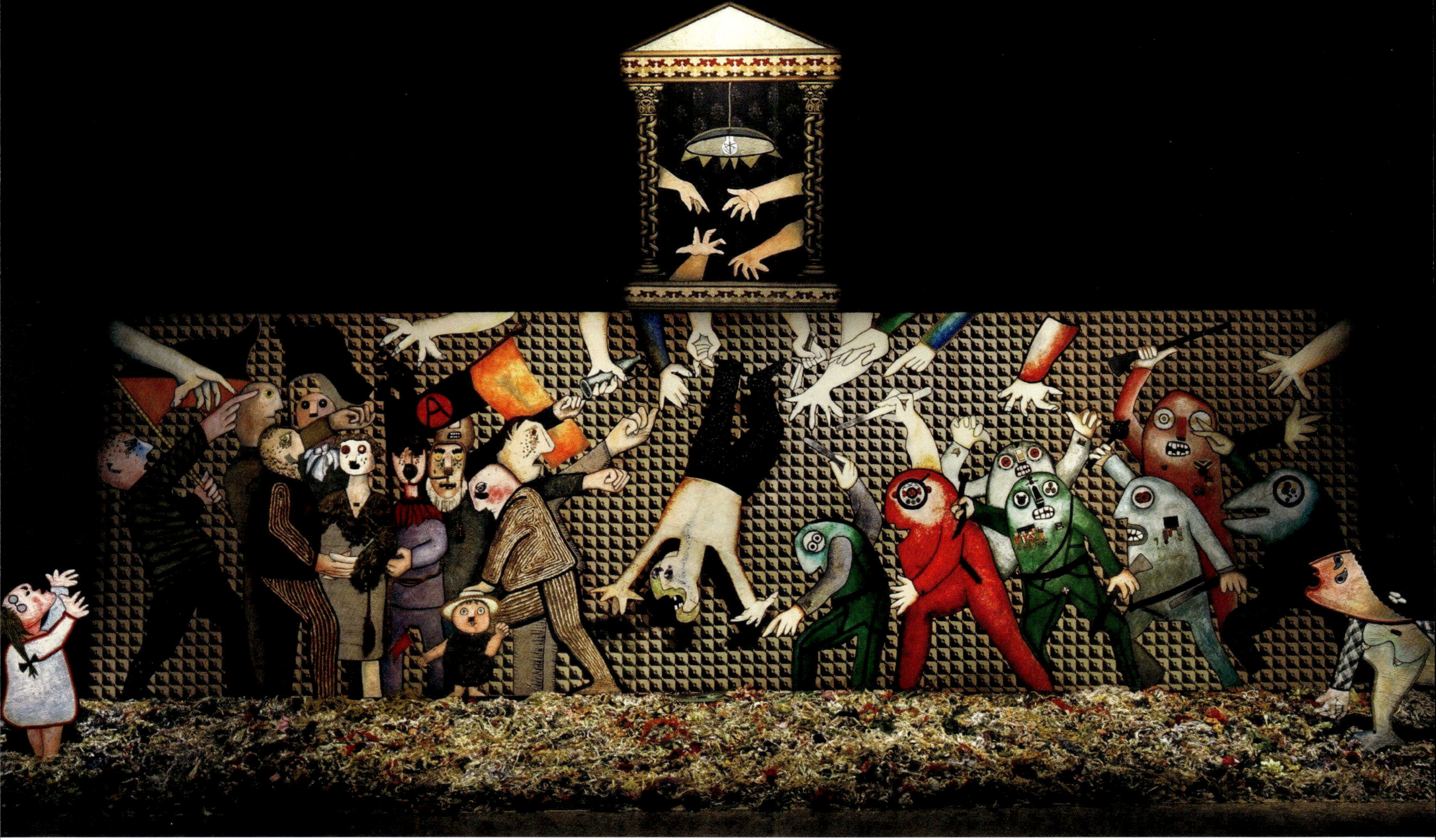

He was best known for his Generals: the farcical authority figures, bloviate and over-decorated, that for Enrico Baj – self-declared 'Nuclear Artist' – represented the idiocy of the Second World War and the corrupt influences that thrived in its wake. But it was another explosion, far closer to home, that prompted the largest work he ever made – and for which he was robustly censored.

On the 12th December 1969, a bomb went off in a bank on the Piazza Fontana in central Milan, killing 17 bystanders and injuring several dozen more. At a time of great civil unrest and public demonstrations by leftwing activists, local police did not look far (or long) before drawing up a list of suspects. Giuseppe Pinelli was one of several members of the Anarchist Black Cross group picked up by the carabiniere for questioning (without evidence). Three days later, during an interrogation, Pinelli was seen falling out of the fourth-floor window of the police station to his death.

It would take more than 15 years before Pinelli and his fellow anarchists were officially cleared. One activist, Pietro Valpreda, spent three years in jail before the police finally relented and released him. The bomb, it was later discovered, had likely been the act of the Ordine Nuovo, one of several neo-Fascist terror groups active in Italy in the 1970s and '80s. But Pinelli's 'accidental' denefestration under police custody sparked immediate and nationwide condemnation. When offered a potential exhibition space, the anarchic Baj saw an opportunity to make a statement of his own.

The Funeral of the Anarchist Pinelli (1972), pictured above, memorialises (and satirises) not Pinelli's funeral but the very moment of his death. Its title references the Futurist Carlo Carra's 1910 painting of the violent suppression of the funeral of Angelo Galli, a picket leader who was stabbed to death by factory guards. But its obvious debts are to Picasso. To the left, Baj joins Pinelli's family, journalists, and outraged citizens; to the right, police in the guise of Baj's famous generals, tadpole-like and bristling with medals, ready to pounce on the condemned Pinelli; and between them, the plunging figure of Pinelli himself, thrown by anonymous hands from a window illuminated by a lamp lifted straight out of *Guernica*.

Baj's mural installation was to be exhibited in the atmospheric Hall of the Caryatids at the Palazzo Reale in Milan, famously fire-bombed by the British during the Second World War and the very same space where Picasso's *Guernica* had toured in 1953. Part of the fabrication he undertook in the nearby headquarters of another Anarchist group Pinelli had affiliated with. But by a freak

Above: *The Funeral of the Anarchist Pinelli*, 1972
Opposite: Enrico Baj in his studio with *Mirrors*, Milan, 1960 © Attilio Bacci

coincidence, on 17th May, 1972, Luigi Calabresi, the Comissioner responsible for Pinelli's detention, was shot dead by a leftwing extremist. The promoters of the exhibition closed ranks; the show was immediately, and indefinitely, called off: at the time, the anarchists were still unofficially held responsible for the Piazza Fontana attack. It would take an extraordinary 28 years before Baj's mural was shown again, and another 20 still before it found a permanent home in Milan's public gallery.

The decade that followed the Pinelli affair was later dubbed the *Anni di Piombo* – the 'Years of Lead': a chapter in Italian history marked by violent kidnappings and terrorist plots, from both extremes of the political spectrum. The name seemed particularly apt where Baj was concerned – as if the lead casing holding back the boiling tensions of the new Atomic era had exploded from the pressure behind it, unleashing powerful waves of radiation affecting society at every level.

Baj was not alone in attempting to piece together some kind of response to these problems – tensions between the industrial, republican north of his home county, and a less prosperous, loyalist, monarchist south; the disentanglement of colonial stations; corruption rushing to fill the power vacuum left by the turmoil of the war. Italian artists reacted with equal variety. Some looked to French and American abstraction, disavowing the human figure; others turned instead to the past, returning to the symbolism of Italy's ancient history. But for Baj, a new era demanded a new kind of art: one that fundamentally changed our relationship with the material world, as the A-bomb had, and that did so with furious anger, wit and hope for change. Look closely at his Pinelli

'No academic prejudice can any longer impose the exclusive or dogmatic use of only oil paints or watercolours. Every material, in fact, is colour, every object. And these objects are frequently much more authentic than the colours that get squeezed out of a tube...'

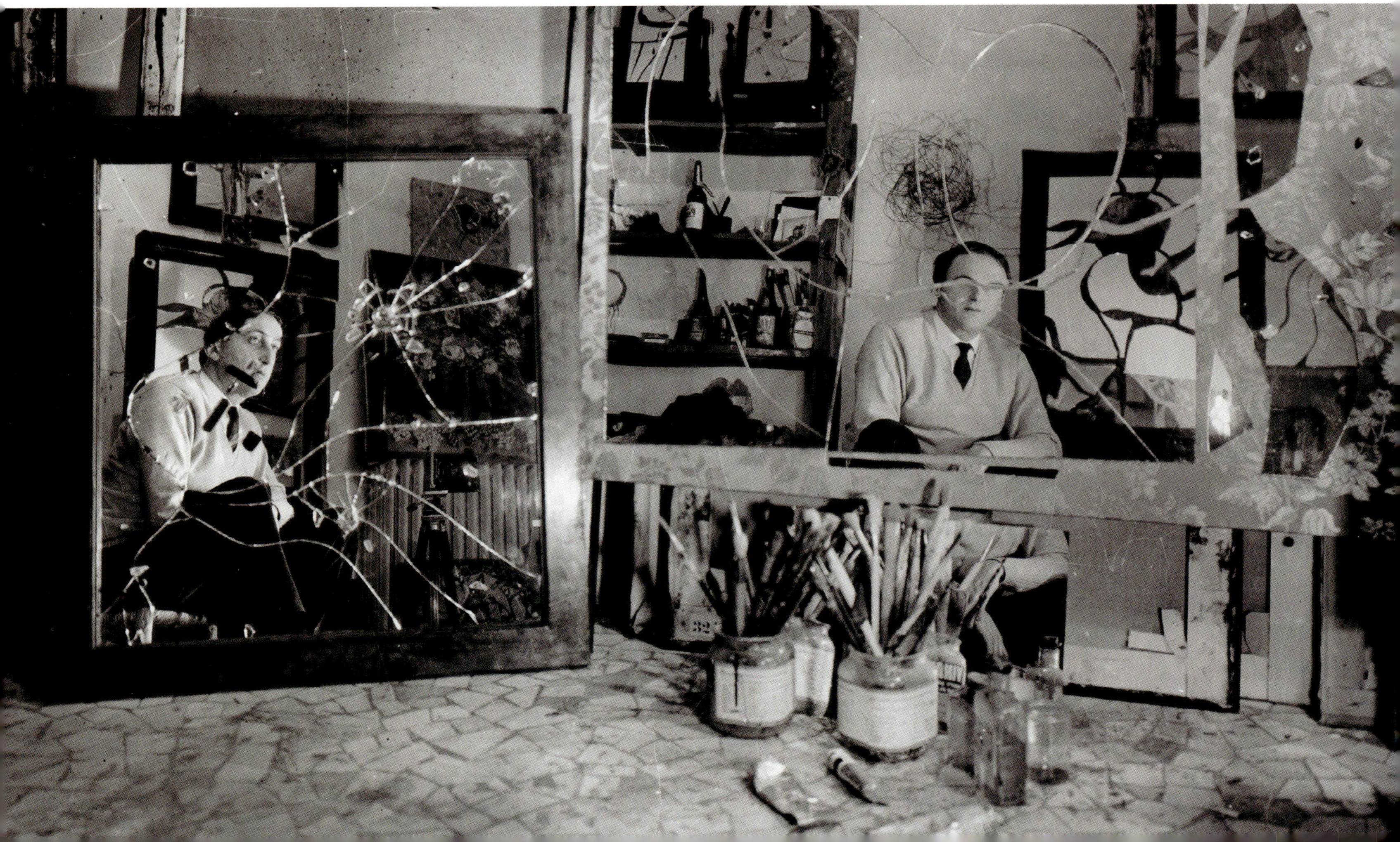

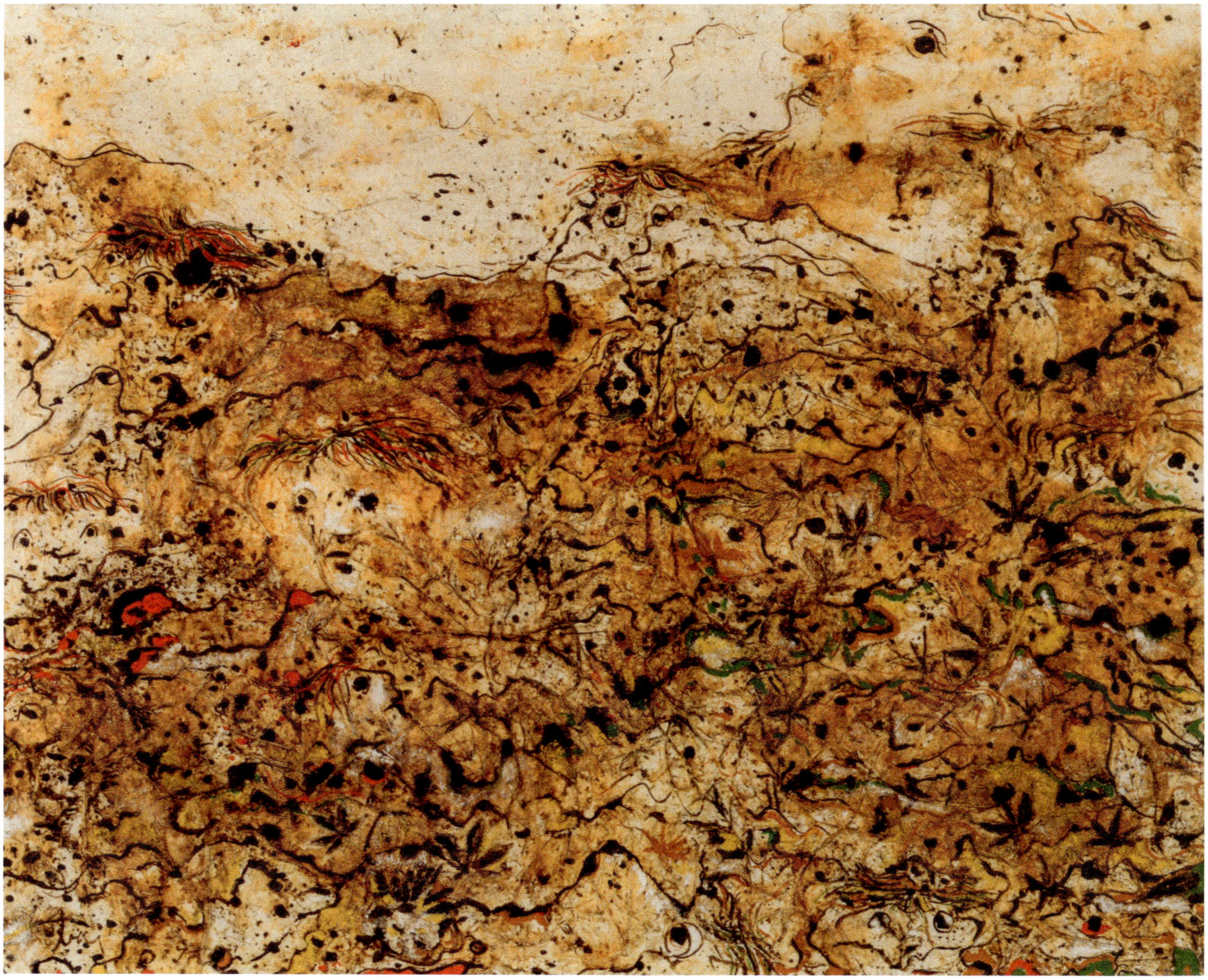

installation and you'll see the scrappy, reconstitutive character of Baj's art: cotton rags and fabric oddments, figures painted on removable boards, studded with buttons, belts and medals; 'painting' with objects in the third dimension.

Born in 1924 in Lombardy, Baj may have inherited his bricolage skills from his parents, both of them engineers, his mother being the first woman to graduate from the Politecnico di Milano. He revealed his disruptive nature early as a boy, mocking the fascist police of Mussolini's Italy and refusing to take part in propaganda exercises. The young Baj thought he might change the world first as a doctor, then a lawyer, before settling on becoming an artist. In 1951 he made his first splash with an exhibition announcing the arrival of *Arte Nucleare* – 'Nuclear Art', a movement that vowed to do away with cool rationalisation and abstraction and instead confront the global aftershock of the Second World War head on.

Like Dada, arriving on the heels of a tremendous fracturing of European society during the First World War, Nuclear Art was born in the wake of a worldwide devastation. For Baj, all semblance of human civility had died in the gas chambers in Auschwitz, the fires at Dresden, the excruciating evaporation of thousands upon thousands under Little Boy and Fat Man in Hiroshima and Nagasaki. Man's capacity for self-destruction had proved limitless. Unsurprisingly, where reasonable methods had failed, he turned instead to irrational influences for his art: Alfred Jarry and his perverse, satirical Pataphysics, the pseudo-science of 'imaginary solutions'; the cannibalistic collage techniques of Max Ernst; the wry commentary of Duchamp, who would become a close friend; the unyielding desire

price guide inside back cover

to disrupt of arch-Surrealist André Breton, a future champion of Baj's work.

As far as Enrico Baj and his younger co-founder, Sergio Dangelo, were concerned, the detonation of the A-Bomb had unleashed a power orders of magnitude beyond anything that had come before it – a power that had wiped out all relevance of 'academic "isms"'. In its wake, painting could and must be fashioned anew. 'Forms disintegrate,' the Nuclearists' first manifesto declared: 'man's new forms are those of the atomic universe; the forces are electrical charges. Ideal beauty is no longer the property of a stupid hero-caste, nor of the "robot". But it coincides with the representation of nuclear man and his space. Truth is not yours, it lies in the ATOM.'

What exactly were these 'new forms'? And what did an 'atomic truth' look like for the Nuclear Artists – among them colleagues from the recently disbanded COBRA group, like the Danish artist Asger Jorn, and new kids on the block, neo-Dadaists and conceptualists Yves Klein and Piero Manzoni?

For Baj, there could be no retreating into pretty geometries, abstract decorations, or anything coolly intellectual. His first images of Nuclear art were decidedly literal: black, voluminous mushroom clouds that appear to transform into charred and nightmarish figures, suggestive of the profoundly distressing naïve drawings made by the survivors of Hiroshima and Nagasaki. By the later 1950s, he had moved onto the Mountains series, bleak, ragged landscapes, made from drips of a tarry black paint dribbled over layers of discarded fabric and a thinned emulsion that Baj liked to call his 'heavy water'. Look closely and you can see tiny little faces woven into their rockfaces – much of Baj's art plays on this *pareidolia*, a natural tendency to see human faces and figures in our inanimate surroundings.

But his most enduring series remains the Generals and Ladies – a series, ironically, that appears at first glance like a cast of 'stupid heroes and robots'. These portraits

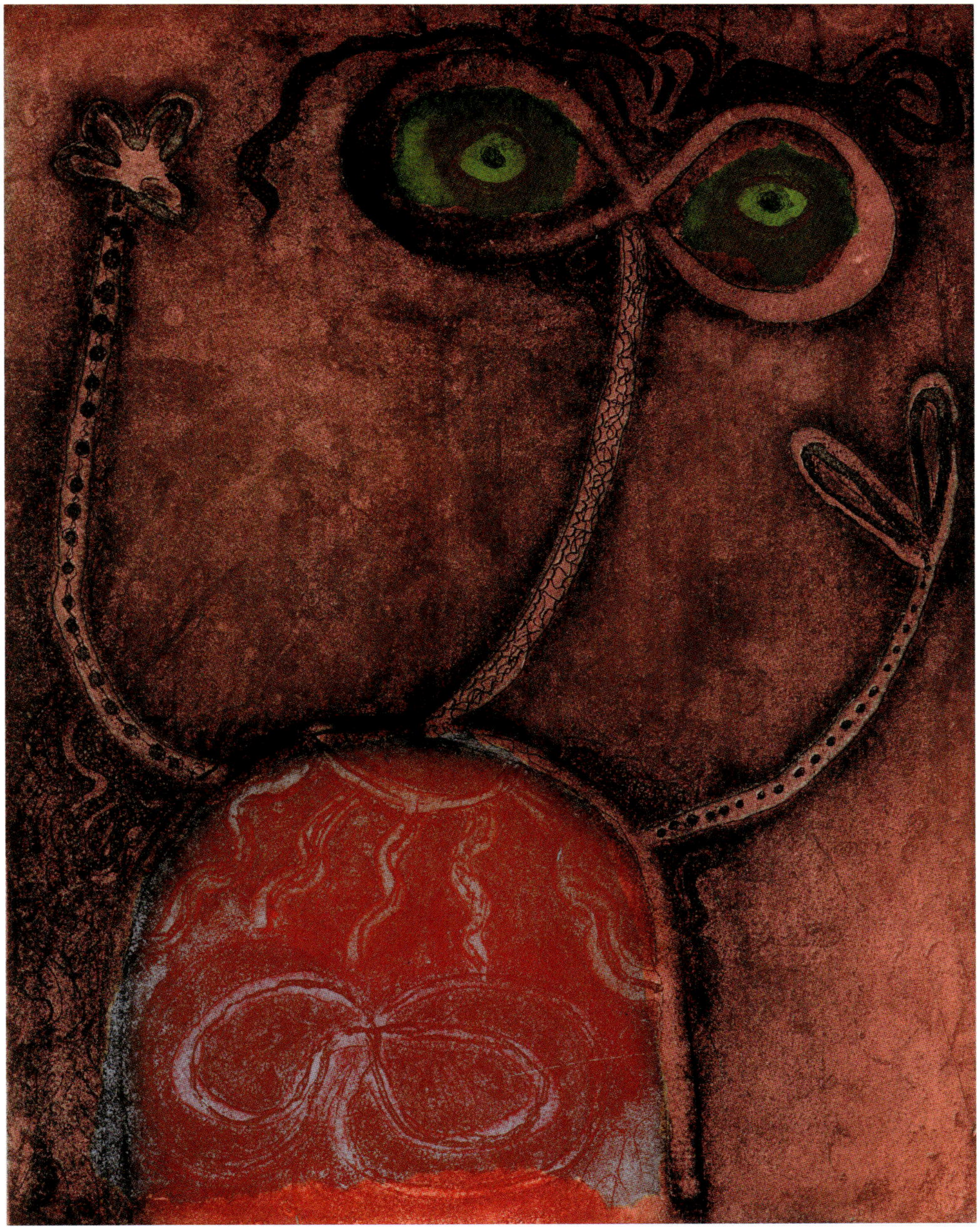

Opposite: *Montagna*, 1957
Above: *Faire des pieds et des Mains* from *Dames et Généraux*, etching, 1964

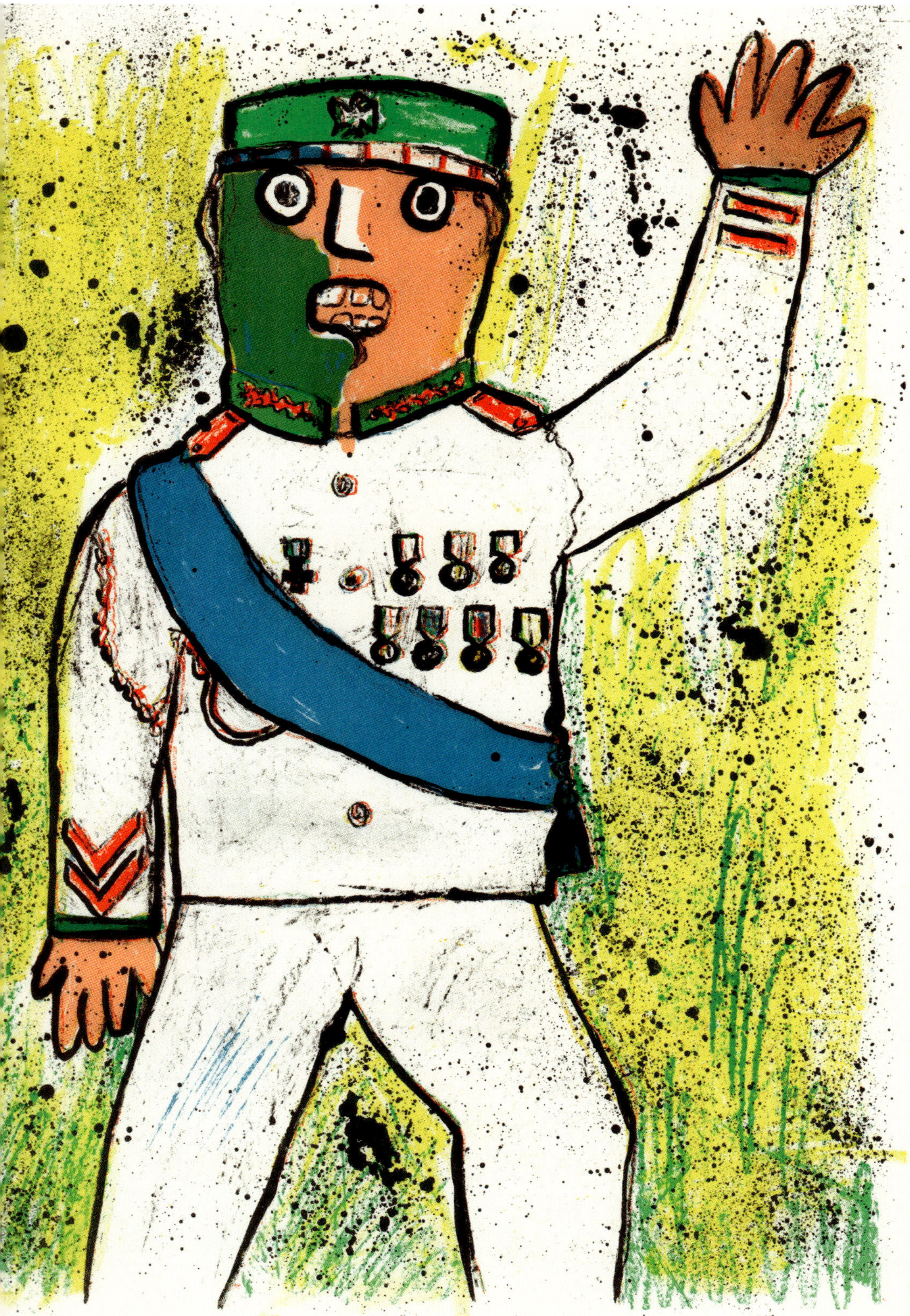

of dehumanised *generalissimi* and wailing dames Baj termed his relief 'paintings', where his 'brushstrokes' could be all manner of detritus – Lego blocks, Meccano, buttons, cork, cotton reels – anything Baj could get his hands on. These archetypal macho figures Baj had modelled on Jarry's infamous King Ubu, but they proved an adaptable allegory for detested political figures of choice – from Nixon and Kissinger to Silvio Berlusconi, whose extraordinary second rise to power Baj witnessed shortly before his death in 2003. Like Berlusconi, King Ubu and his own Generals represented for him 'all the vulgarity and arrogance of power… a machine-king-boss… guarantor and repository of all of the Absurd, of all Irony, of the entire caricature of this adorable and repugnant fin de siecle of ours.'

Regarding the post-war period as an opportunity for a clean break with all that came before, Baj worked with childlike curiosity and total disregard for 'the rules'. He did everything you are not supposed to do, and his work was everything it was not supposed to be: magnificently maximalist, too disdainful for Pop, not marvellous enough for Surrealism. What he saw as the commodification of the art world, and indeed society more broadly, drove him to make copies of other people's paintings – Picasso, Seurat, de Chirico – in his own bizarre and pastiched style. He disparaged a greedy, things-obsessed world with his own greedy, obsessive collecting and rearranging of everyday materials, and laughed at the contradiction. He decried kitsch, but there was a kitsch-lite heart to his own work: a refusal to take himself too seriously, and to make the very manufacture of his assemblages reflective of the ineffectual, patchwork problem solving of the 20th century.

Most sacrilegious of all, Baj dared to be *fun*. Illustrated throughout this article are print-collages from a suite entitled *La Cravate ne vaut pas une medaille* – 'The tie is not worth a medal', a comment on the hollow

Above: *Untitled (General)*, lithograph, 1964
Opposite top: *Untitled* from *La Cravate ne Vaut pas une Médaille*, screenprint & collage, 1972
Opposite bottom: *A Mi-Chemin*, from *Dames et Généraux*, etching, 1964

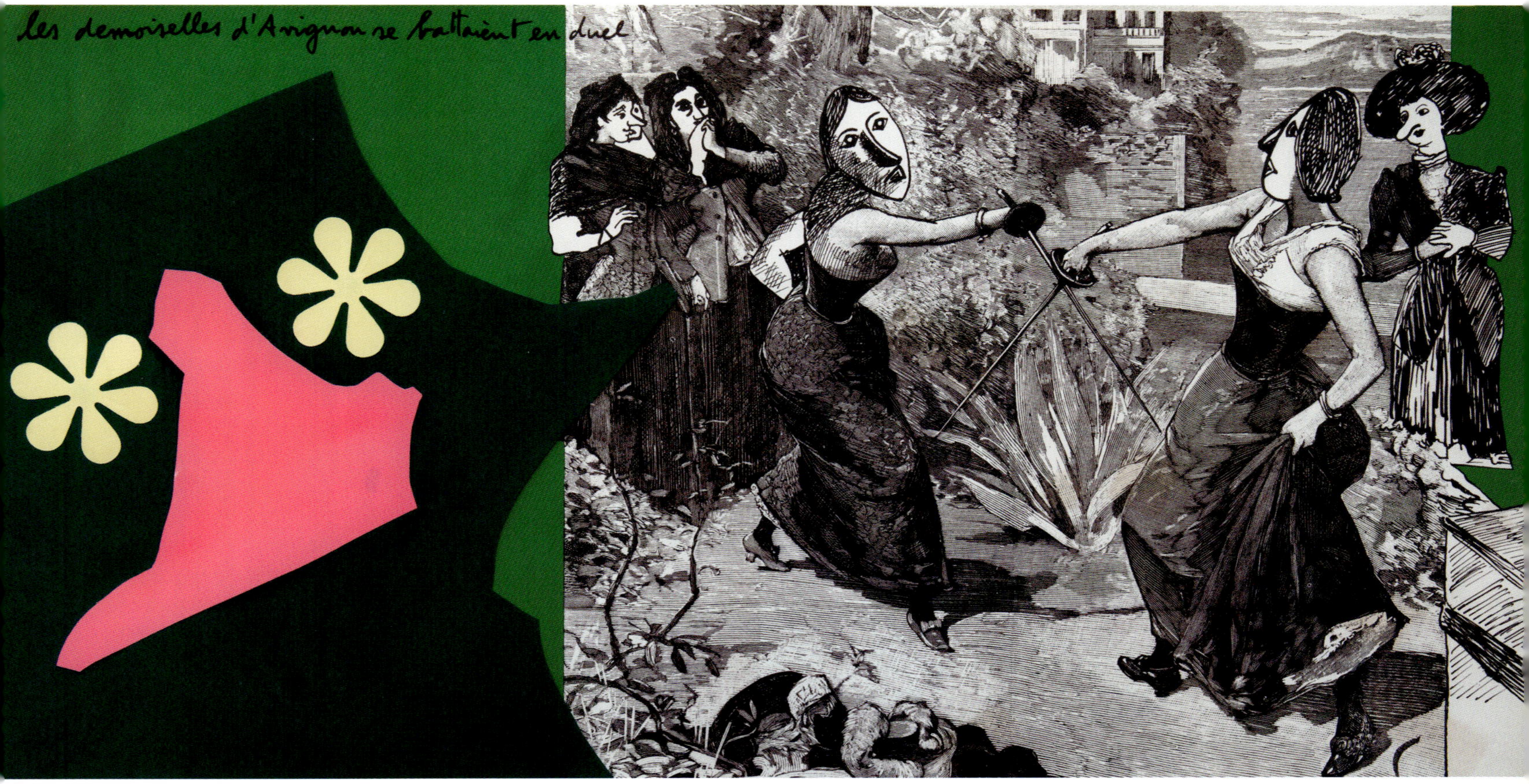

virtues of military trophies and the seepage of fascist thought into the corporate world. Made in 1972, the series, which combines screenprinting with plastic collaged elements and stickers, arrived on the heels of the Pinelli episode. At first glance they seem a welcome, playful reprieve after a period of intense scrutiny. But the message of the Generals is still there, masked behind clownish plastic faces grinning ludicrously behind bow ties or screaming their orders to the skies.

In 1957 Baj released another manifesto, issuing an ultimatum to his contemporaries making tasteful abstract patterns: 'Upholsterers or painters: you have to choose…every canvas is a changing scene of an unpredictable commedia dell'arte. We affirm the unrepeatable nature of the work of art.'

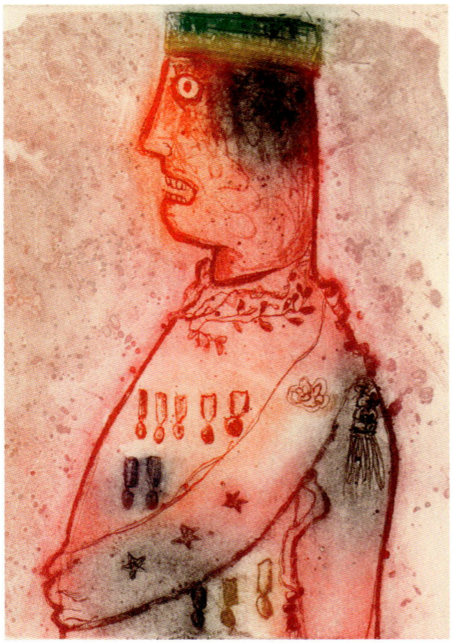

'Wars, generals, decorations, wounds, amputations. As consolation the motherland gives you a few pretty coloured ribbons and maybe a medal that bears the inscription "smelted from the bronze of the enemy." All madness. Total madness.'

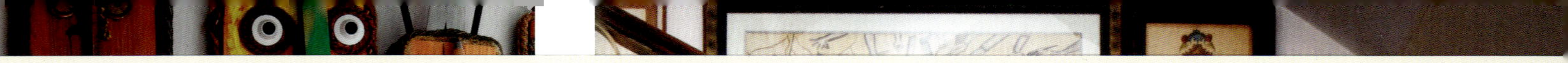

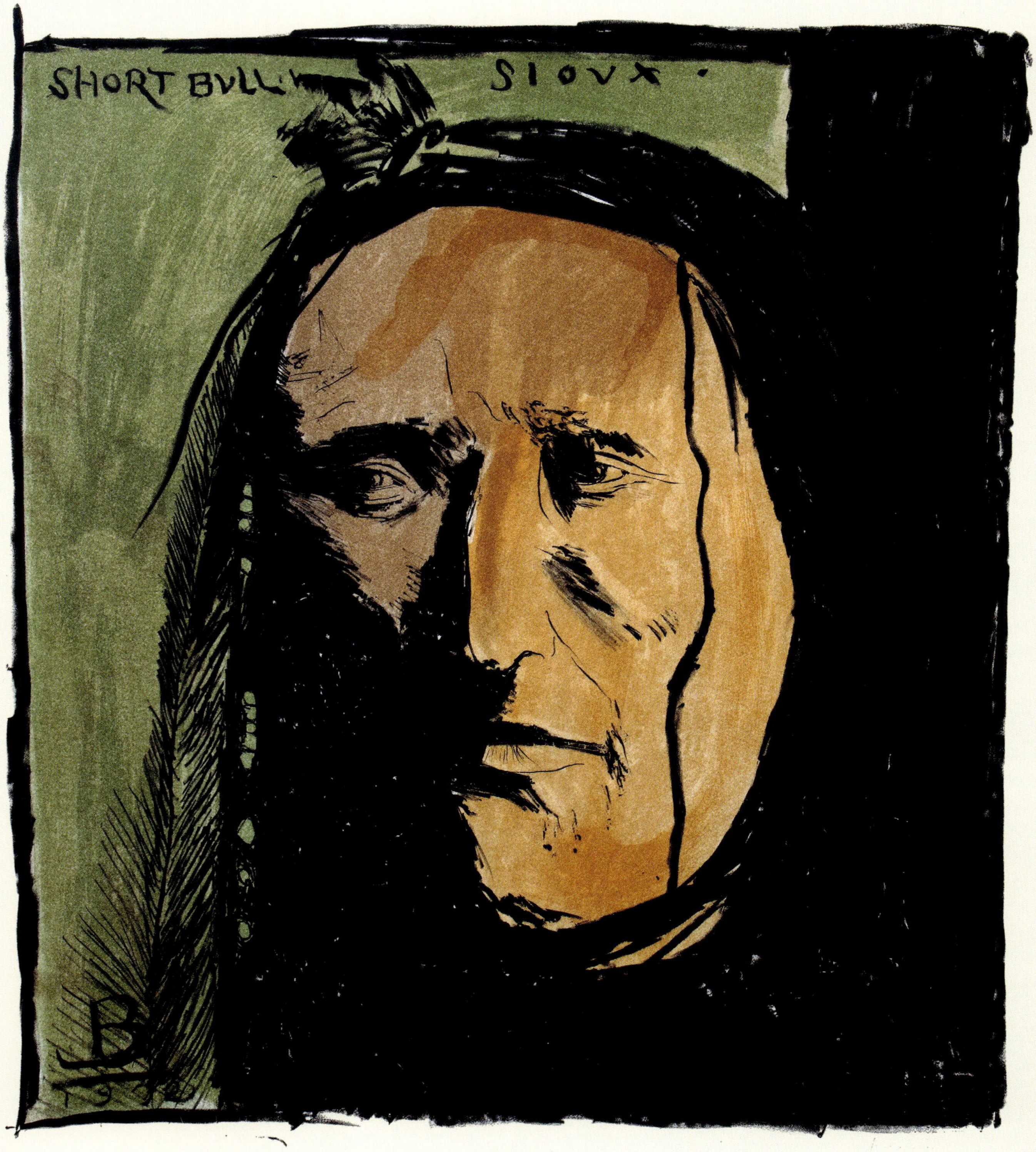
SHORT BULL
SIOUX

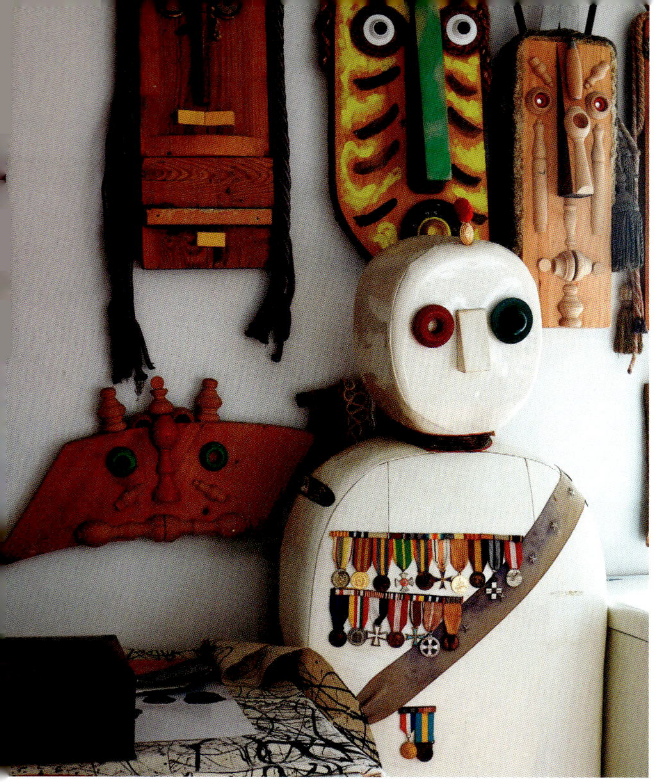
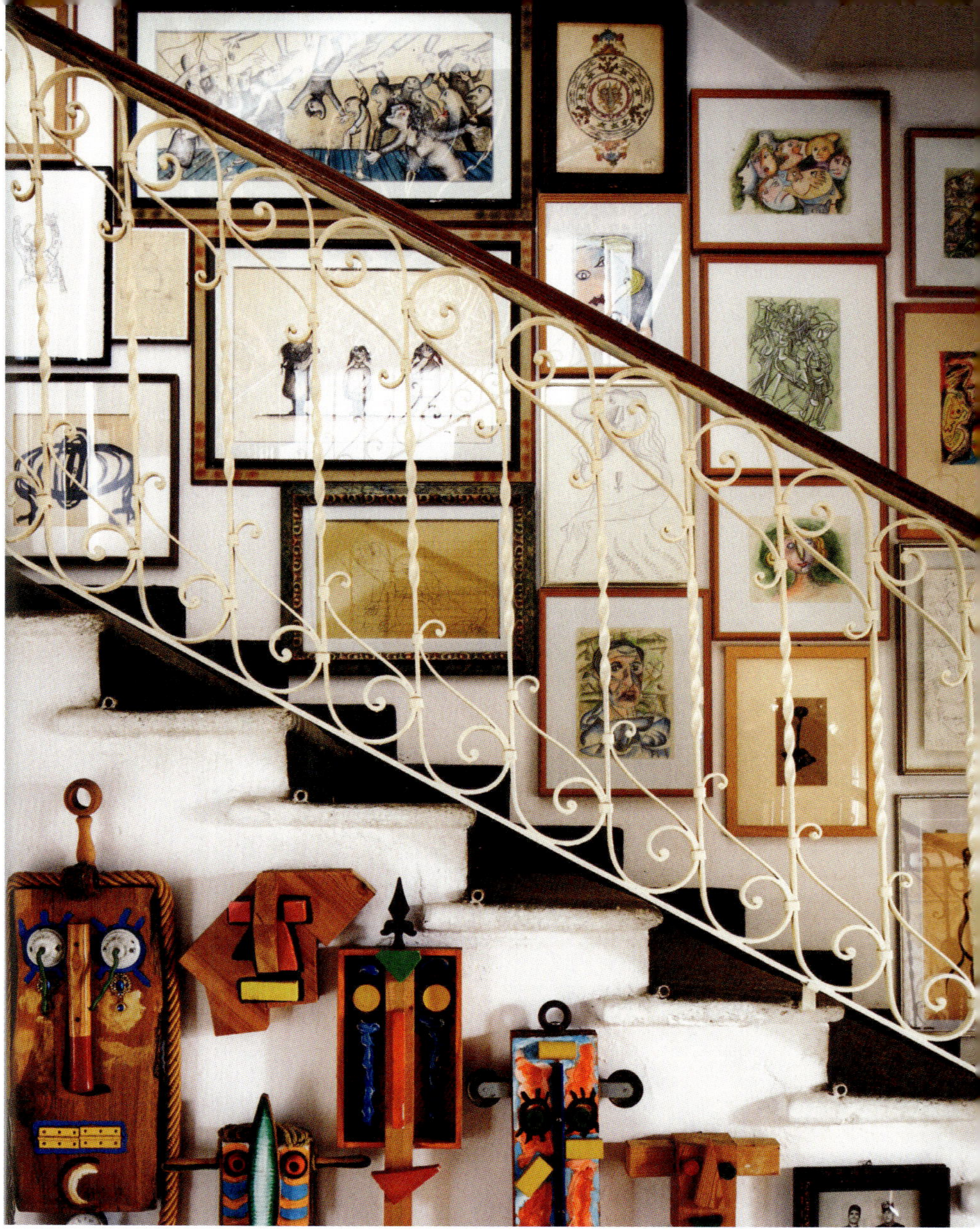
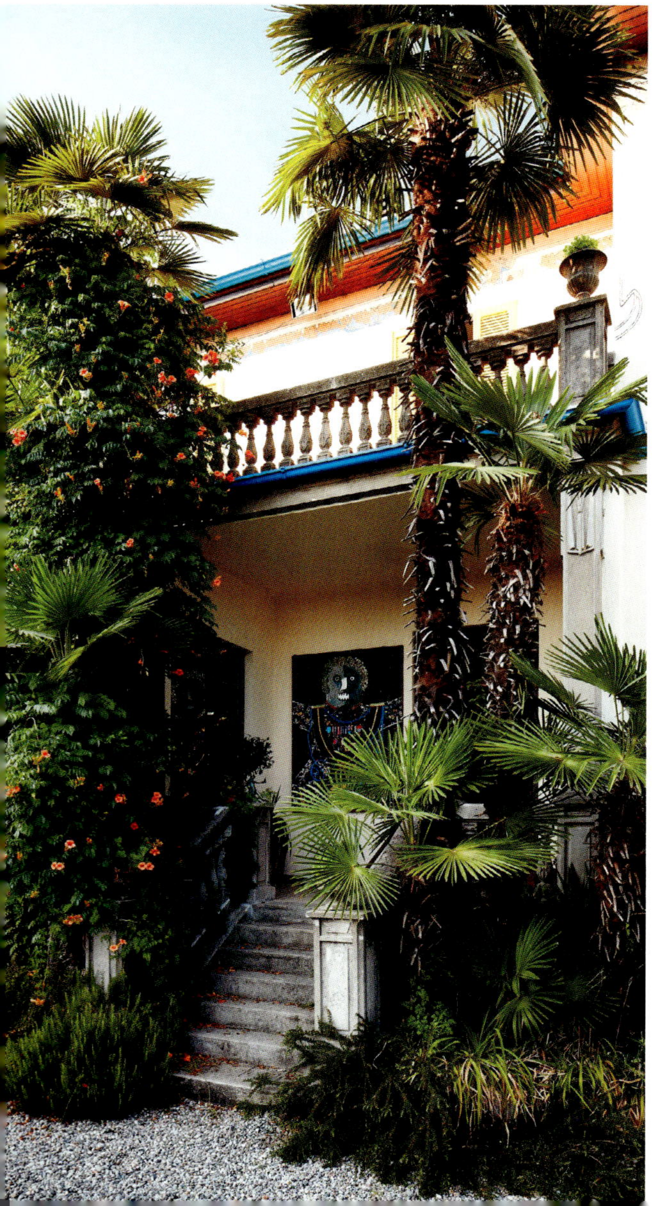
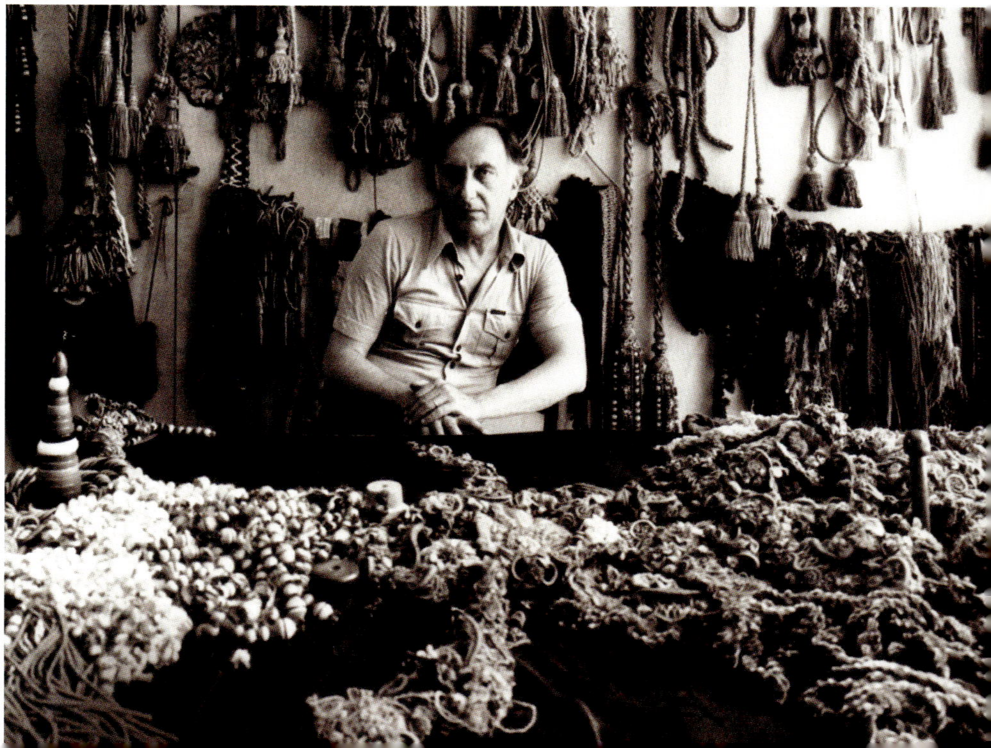

He seemed unaware of, or unconcerned with the irony of using upholstery as an insult while painting on fabrics and discarded furnishings. And though he denounced predictable repetition, with series like the Generals, who returned time and again in various guises, their power depended on the very notion of repetition, like a slogan-caller at a rally. But to get a sense of what Baj's forever changing and unpredictable definition of art should be, we only have to look to his house in Vergiate, in the aristocratic north of Italy: an Art Nouveau-style mansion, rescued by Baj and his wife, Roberta, from an over-enthusiastic garden in 1967.

Its interior – meticulously photographed by Stephen Kent Johnson for a publication dedicated to Baj and the house in 2017 – reveals the mind of an exceptional eccentric. Like the late Joe Tilson, who had his own love affair with Italy, Baj prized furniture: drawers, compartments, wardrobes, the idea of putting things in their place (in more than one sense of the phrase). On the walls hang veneer facades of imagined draws, scarcely a few millimetres thick, bristling, frame-edge to frame-edge, with a wealth of pictures, drawings and prints that served as a kind of cultural currency between Baj and his fellow artists (I can spot a Wifredo Lam and an André Masson on the wall that have passed through the gallery's hands on more than once occasion). This beautiful house he filled almost as a riposte to its original coolness and grandeur. Every room is an assembly, displaying the results of expeditions to bric-a-brac boutiques in nearby Milan and Paris. He and Roberta would ransack hardware shops, tailors and haberdasheries for new materials – so many medals, ribbons and tassels that they were occasionally forced to buy extra suitcases to get them home. This surfeit of material was neatly squirreled away in boxes and filing cabinets, along with the vast archive of letters, all kept by Roberta, that testify to the huge number of contacts and collaborations Baj made and the terrific energy he brought to all that he did.

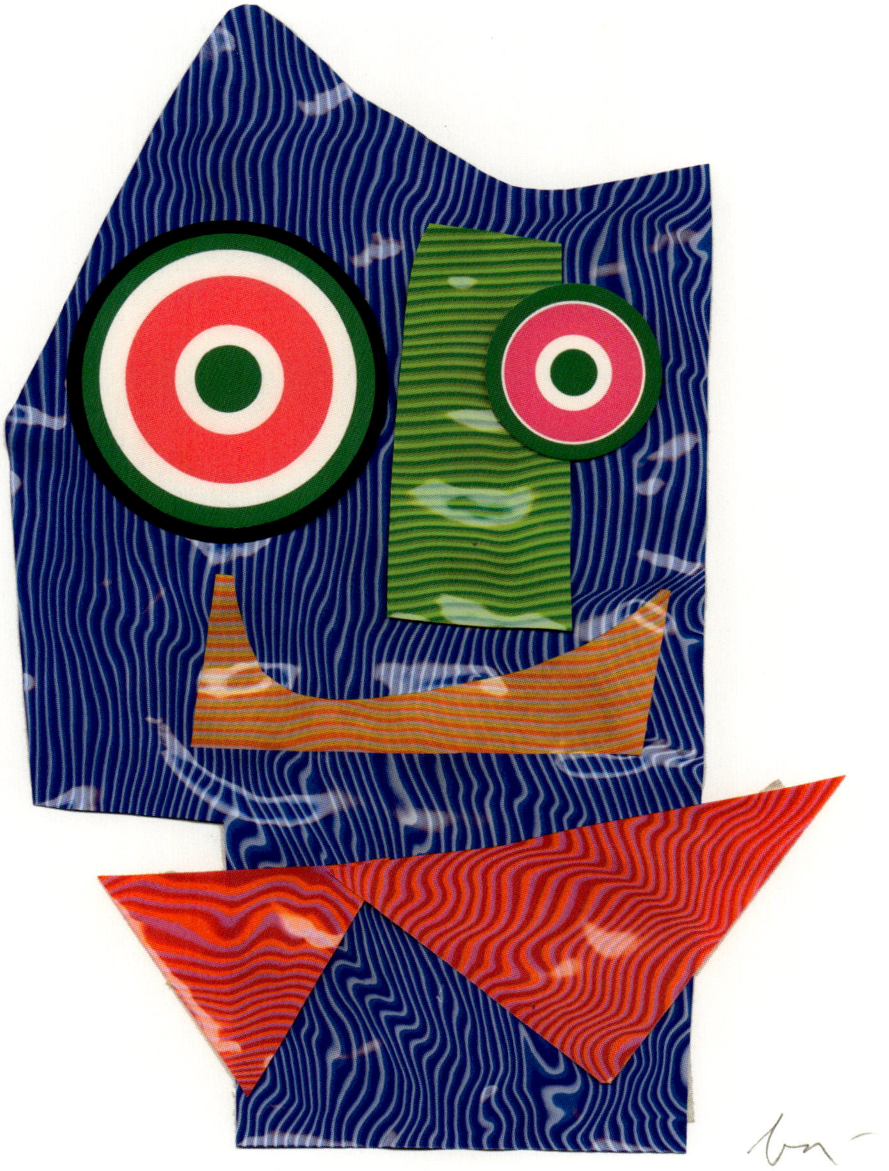

Baj's work was ultimately about power, its absurdity, its fragility, its corruptibility – all aspects contained and reflected in the art itself. Like all court jesters, he danced on the line separating comedy and tragedy – there is an element of wilful hysteria about his screaming generals and disembodied ladies, all flinging spaghetti arms and eyes on stalks. He concentrated wit and parody in the fabrication of powerful figures from the everyday and the discardable; the Emperor's new clothes were, in fact, nothing more than bottle caps, curtain tassels and tin foil. But he also seemed to want to say there is great beauty in these constituent parts – things people leave behind. That, after all, is the difficulty with power, its instruments, its trophies: they repulse and beguile in equal measure. We only wish we might be special enough not to succumb to them.

Opposite: Enrico Baj's home in Vergiate, © Stephen Kent Johnson for Skira Rizzoli
Opposite bottom right: Enrico Baj in his studio in Vergiate, 1975 © Aurelio Amendola
Above: *Untitled* from *La Cravate ne Vaut pas une Médaille*, collage, 1972

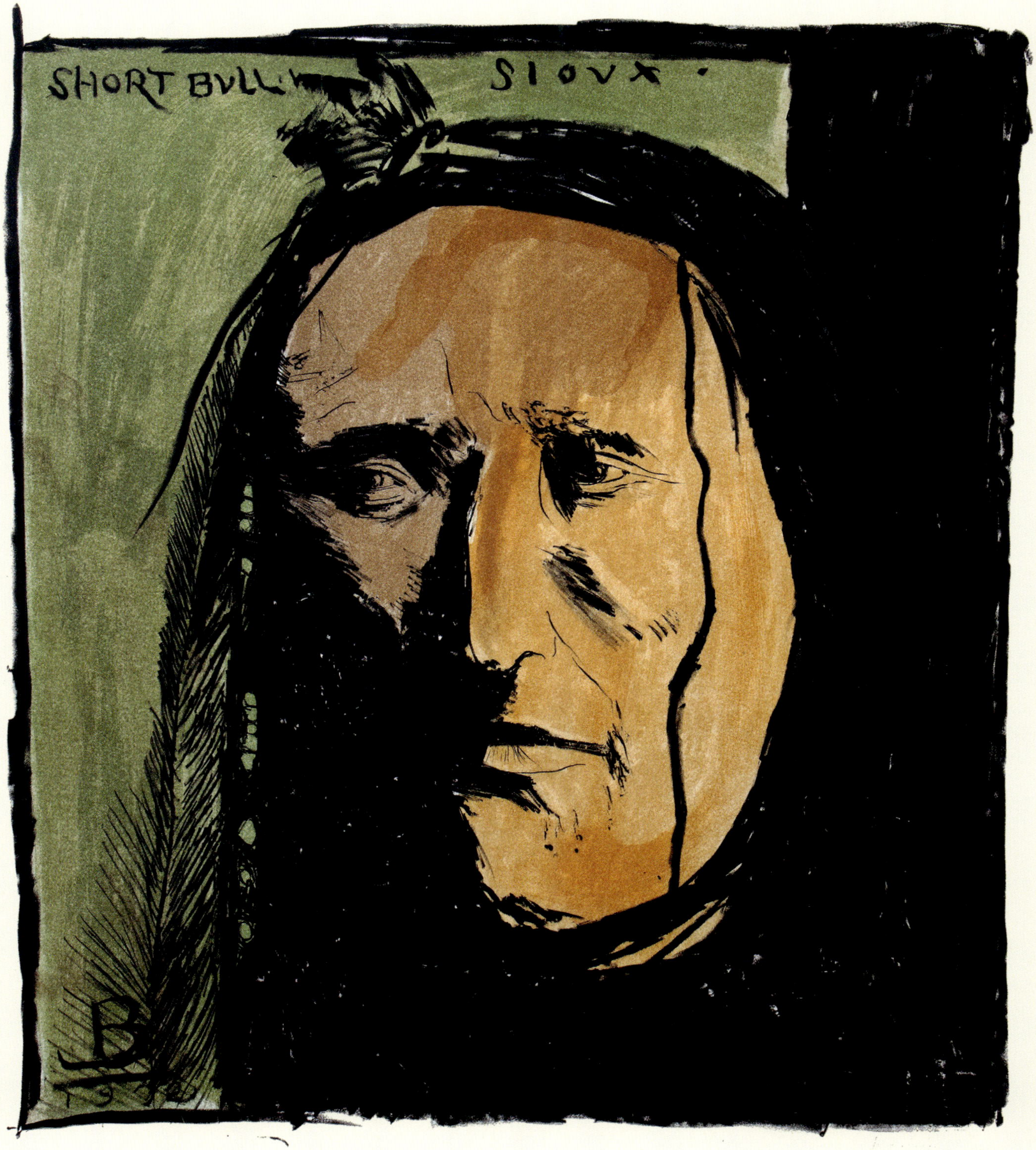
SHORT BULL
SIOUX

LEONARD BASKIN

The Native American Portraits

A commission from the National Park Service led the sculptor and printmaker Leonard Baskin to a lifelong fascination with American Indian history – and a series of portraits that rank among the artist's most moving.

As the clocks struck midnight on 4th July, 1876, fireworks shot overhead at Independence Hall in Philadelphia, where gathered the great and the good of American society to celebrate the country's 100th birthday. While rocket bursts illuminated the crowds below, hundreds of miles away telegraph operators hastily relayed a message that would soon put an end to the festivities: General George Armstrong Custer, dreamboy commander of the 7th Cavalry and hero of the frontier, lay naked and dead with all 200 and more of the men under his command, slain by a coalition of Native Indian tribes on the elevated grasslands of Little Bighorn River.

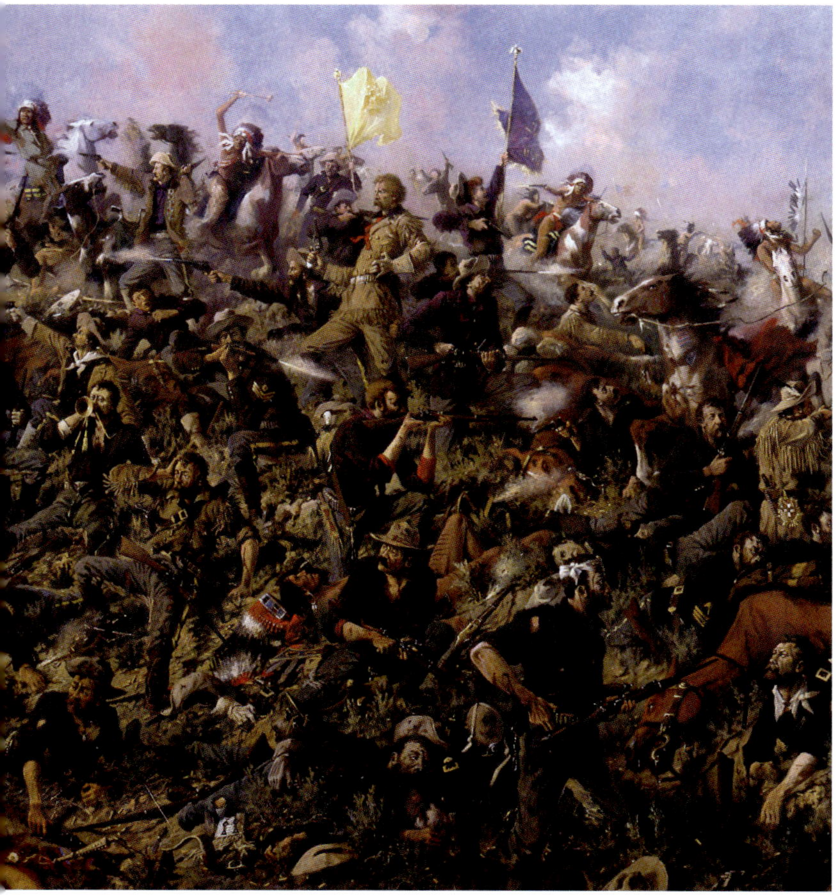

To understand the curious hold the legend of Custer had on the American popular imagination, you have only to look at the immediate outpouring of reproductions of the event that followed it. By the late 1960s, Mitchell Wilder, director of the Amon Carter Museum in Fort Worth, Texas, described counting close to a thousand different versions of the battle in their picture archives, making 'this sad occasion...the most memorialized single event in American history.' From beer bottle caps, cigarette cards and bumper stickers to preposterously grand oil paintings, almost every one of them focused on the imagined 'realities' of the battle itself: an amassed fray of Indians and Blue Coats, smoking pistols and carbines, and heaps of dead bodies, the panoramic vista of the Montana horizon glimpsed beyond. Here is the familiar blueprint of the great Hollywood western epic: the theatre of man's brutal territorial disputations, dwarfed by a vast landscape otherwise unspoilt by human contact. But the Custer episode has proved special – an event so tightly wrapped up with the great American foundation myth, and the guilt complex at its heart, that popular culture would always find it relevant and meaningful. It comes as no surprise to learn that when the US Army presence in Vietnam hit an all-time high – and public support for the war an all-time low – gritty exploitation films (*Soldier Blue*, 1970; *Ulzana's Raid*, 1972) and picaresque revisionary histories (*Little Big Man*, 1970) looked to the frontier, and to Custer especially, for their allegory of choice: troopers sent to die in an unjustified war, in unfamiliar terrain, against a more experienced guerilla enemy.

In all this noise, the Native American voice was often lost. It was not an Indian artist, but the New Jersey-born and Brooklyn-raised sculptor Leonard Baskin whom Vincent Gleason, publications director of the National Park Service, approached in 1968 to illustrate a new souvenir handbook detailing the events – and the fallout – of the battle at Little Bighorn. Though not native, Baskin's insistence on the importance of figurative art in an era concerned with abstraction made him an ideal candidate, and his talents were prodigious. At 15 he had apprenticed to the sculptor Maurice Glickman before discovering William Blake at Yale. Blake's influence struck him, he remembered, 'like a run-away locomotive. The impact was staggering, irresistible and over-whelming.' He took up etching and woodcuts and, while still a student, established the now-famous Gehenna Press. Named after the valley southwest of Jerusalem, synonymous with hellfire and purgation, it seemed an appropriate imprint for an artist whose work had inherited the dark and angular psychology long evident in Germanic art, from Grünewald and Altdorfer through to Paula Modersohn Becker and Kathe Kollwitz.

Previous page: *Short Bull*, lithograph, c. 1973
Above left: Edgar S. Paxson, *Custer's Last Stand*, oil on canvas (detail), 1899

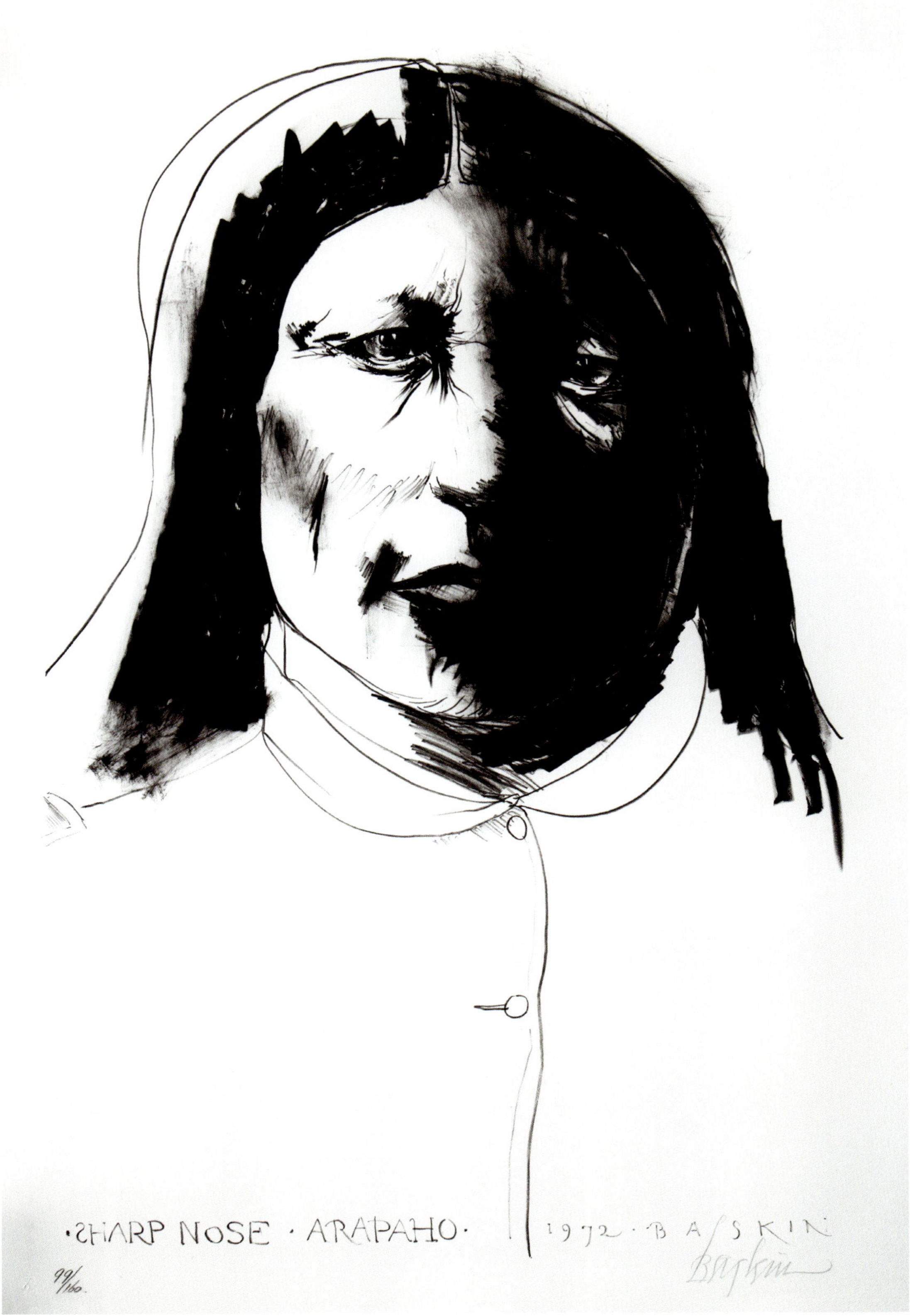

Sharp Nose, Arapaho

A war chief and Indian scout. Sharp Nose commanded the detachment of Native scouts in General Mackenzie's winter campaign against the Cheyenne in November 1876. His son was sent for education (and assimilation) to Carlisle Indian School, Pennsylvania, which boasted to be 'the ultimate Americanizer.' Here he wears his US Army captain's bars.

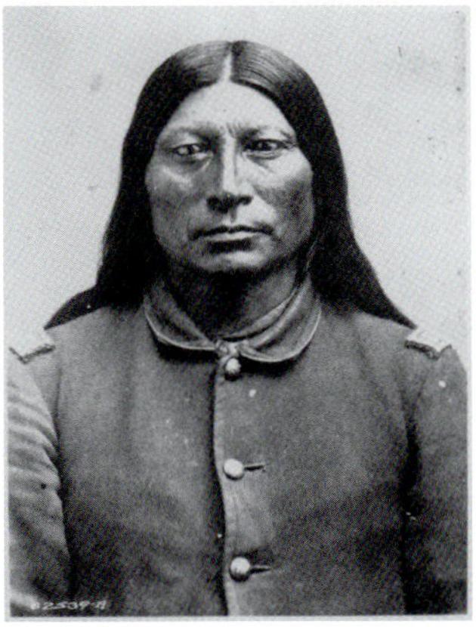

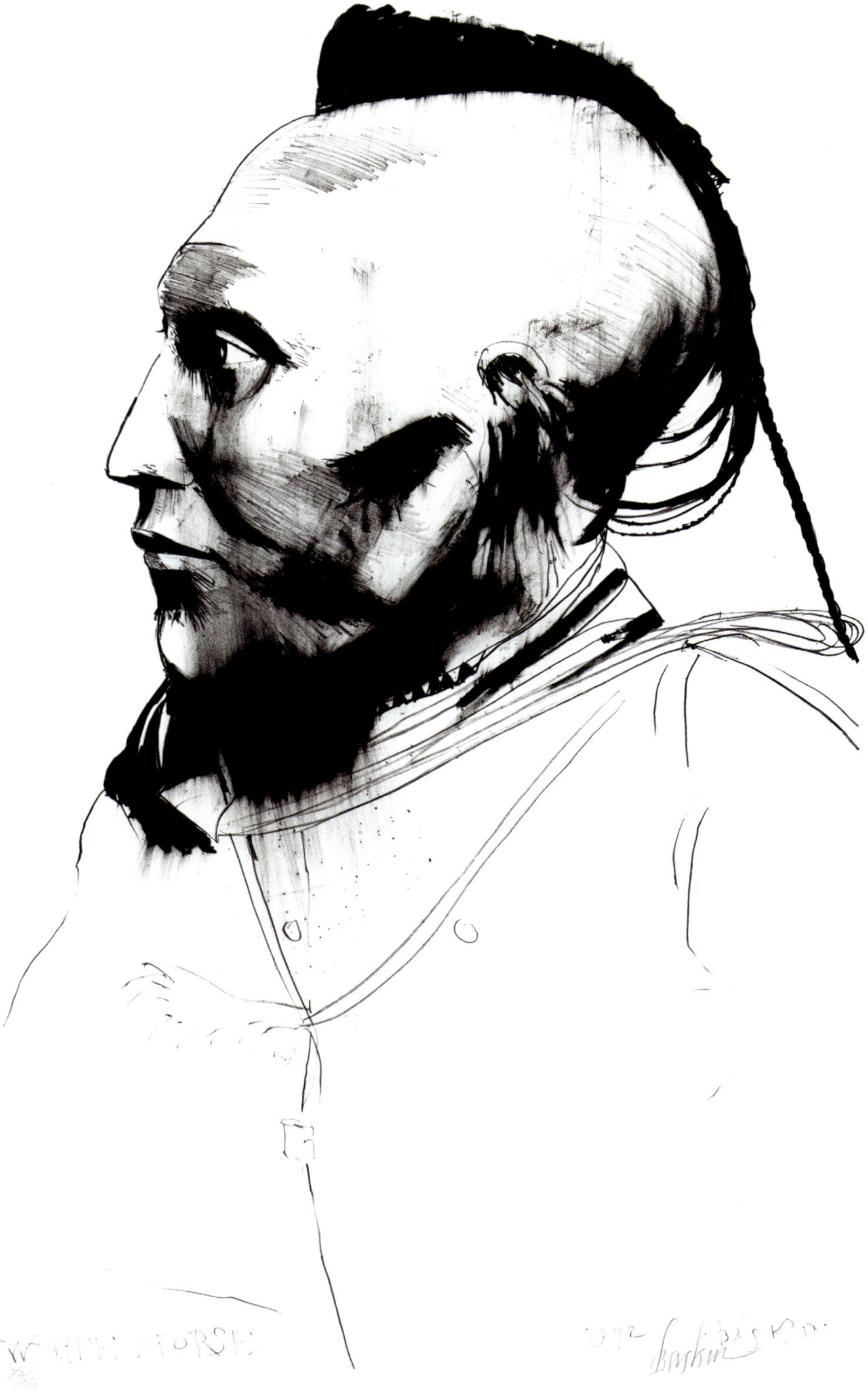

White Horse, Pawnee

From 1866, US Army Quartermasters were authorised to enlist Native scouts (and arm them) to provide navigation, as interpreters, and to protect moving convoys through Native American lands. White Horse wears his hair in a traditional 'roach' or Mohawk.

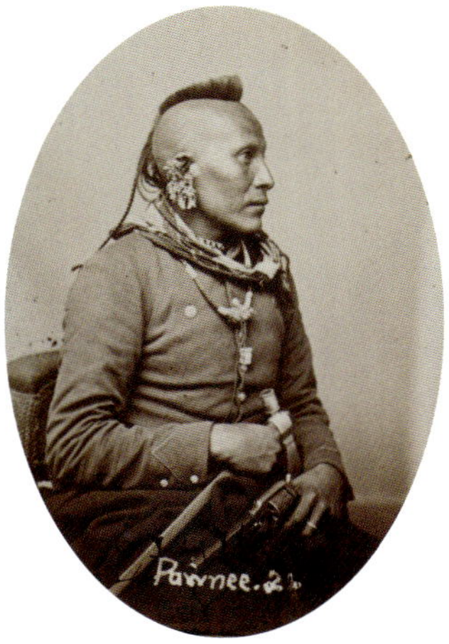

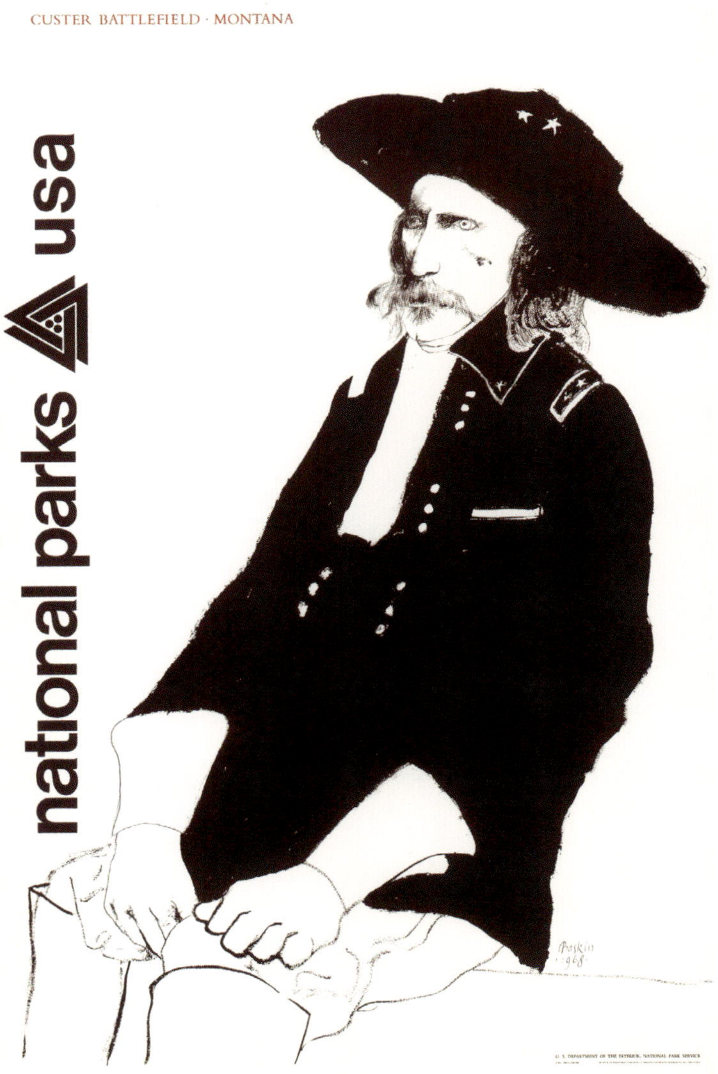

Above: National Parks Custer Battlefield Poster, 1968, with illustration by Leonard Baskin

But what drew him to this unusual project was precisely that sense of historical continuity, a desire to make the past actors of the Bighorn as present as possible. To an audience of fellow printmakers at the American Institute of Graphic Arts a few years before, he had reaffirmed his dedication to the human condition as the ultimate subject, and the human figure as its eternal vehicle: 'I have an exhilarating and oppressive vision of man as immutable, intact and practically unalterable. I could have walked with Socrates, hauled stones for Chartres, set type for Bodoni, and had my skull cracked by a cossack's club in any of innumerable pogroms. I am joined to that colossal continuum of man thrusting through the centuries.'

Baskin knew little of the Plains Indians' history when he accepted the commission. He found in Custer a simultaneously fascinating and repugnant protagonist, awed by 'his sense of posturing, his sense of dressing up, his incredible mania about himself.' But he soon realised that what he had been asked to address was not, as the battle was commonly known, Custer's Last Stand, but that of the Natives who defeated him. With their success at Little Bighorn, the Sioux and Cheyenne coalition had won the battle but lost the war. Retribution from the white man was swift and terrible, ensuring the end of the old ways in the Black Hills and beyond. What began as a series of portraits of the main players in the Bighorn affair – Custer, Sitting Bull, leader of the defiant Sioux, and their colleagues – sparked an interest in other forgotten Native leaders. Baskin continued to produce drawings and lithographic portraits into the '70s and beyond: prints, watercolours, and hand-bound books, right into the last decade of his life.

The son of a rabbi and brother of two more, Baskin was not the first Jew to become interested in the plight of the American Indian. A full 50 years before the battle of Little Bighorn itself, the former diplomat Mordecai Manuel Noah – half Ashkenazi, half Portuguese Sephardic, and a prominent public figure in New York – sought to establish a utopian Zion on Grand Island in the Niagara River. Natives were invited to create a new society with his fellow Jewish citizens: Noah was one of many who subscribed to the eccentric theory that Native Americans were descendants of one of the ten Lost Tribes of Israel.

A vague and otherwise superficial 'otherness' shared between Native and Jewish immigrant faces later established the Hollywood tradition of Jewish actors taking Native roles over actual Indians, as gloriously parodied by Mel Brooks' Yiddish-speaking chief in the cult classic *Blazing Saddles* (1974). But Baskin made no mention of his own Jewish roots having informed his approach to Little Bighorn. A curious irony had brought their stories together: each a people without a spiritual home, one indigenous, the other permanently immigrant. Both had, within living memory, faced cultural extinction. The subtext was there for all to see. 'It would be fitful and absurd for me to recount the slaughter, with disease, booze and guns,' Baskin declared of his illustrations; 'but allow me, (in raging haplessness), to indict our government and all of its peoples, not merely for the broken treaties and conventicles, but for allowing Indians to be shut up in reserves, live in penurious degradation, in blight and misery and left to the deadly mercy of the Bureau of Indian Affairs.'

This was a story going back hundreds of years, of course, to the arrival of the first European colonists in the Americas; but the beginning of the end of Native life on the Great Plains could be said to have lain at the Battle of the Little Bighorn.

Like so many stories from the frontier, its catalyst was gold, rumoured to be buried in the Black Hills that were sacred to the Sioux Nation (and other Indians), an alliance of Lakota and Dakota tribes. Settlers had been making deeper incursions into Sioux territory, their railroads penetrating westward with attachments of troops to protect surveyors. The Sioux had themselves been 'invaders' of these lands, pushed westward from Minnesota by their own enemies and then by cessions of land to the United States. Migrating to the Great Plains, they subdued the Cheyenne and displaced smaller tribes like the Crows. By the mid-19th century, accords between the tribes and the US government attempted to halt the steady flow of settlers, but most were made without any intention of enforcing them. But after suffering humiliating defeats at the hands of the Lakota leader Red Cloud, in 1868 US officials drew up the Fort Laramie treaty. On offer was an invitation to establish the Great Sioux reservation: the Black Hills and the surrounding lands would be their exclusive home, with rights to hunt without fear of repression, and federal aid through the winter, ending dependence on the buffalo which were already fast disappearing at the hands of European pelt traders. In exchange, the Sioux would give up vast swathes of their territory – lands formerly promised by older treaties – to accommodate the growing numbers of settlers. Many took up the offer, but several thousand, under the leadership of the charismatic Hunkpapa chief Sitting Bull, refused – among them the fierce Oglala warrior Crazy Horse, an expert raider responsible for many of the US army's worst defeats at the hands of the Natives. They remained adamantly tied to the old ways of Plains life, refusing any negotiation with the white man.

On the opposing side was George Custer. Blond, vivacious, bold – many said to a fault – Custer owed his short but stratospheric career to the Civil War (he lay dead a major general at 25). He quickly climbed the ranks through acts of reckless daring, courted admiration and criticism from his peers, and even made an enemy of President Grant. Like Sitting Bull and Crazy Horse, he had his own experiences of US raiding parties against the Cheyenne near Yellowstone while laying track for the North Pacific Railway.

In 1974 Custer and his infamous 7th Cavalry company were commissioned to explore the Black Hills – land that now lay deep inside the bounds of the Sioux reservation, with the Little Big Horn tributary just beyond. His governing generals wanted to establish a fort nearby, to keep watch on the reservation Indians; but more importantly, local prospectors suspected that untapped seams of gold would be found within the hazy blue peaks. When Custer's expedition returned, they confirmed the rumours were true. A gold rush ensued; attempts to purchase the territory from the Natives were fruitless, thanks to the defiance of Sitting Bull and his own agitators. An air of inevitable catastrophe hung over the Black Hills.

There were striking similarities between the two opposed parties: internal conflicts, rivalries between chiefs and officers alike. The US Army had been quick to exploit the existing tensions between the Sioux and the tribes they had ousted from the Black Hills, recruiting scouts from the Crow, Blackfeet and Pawnee who were only too happy to see their old enemies forced from their lands. Baskin was fascinated especially by the conflicted psychology of these men caught in the middle, their allegiances branded in the Indian naming tradition: the life and striking, painted face of White Man Runs Him, he later wrote, became a personal obsession.

But in the days and weeks before the Little Bighorn battle, Indians from various agencies were spotted converging together, forming a far larger band than any of Custer's superiors had expected, united in grievance at the ongoing desecration of the sacred lands in the hills. What began as a game of cat and mouse, with troopers stalking the travelling camp, soon escalated as the Indian coalition moved along the Yellowstone river. US generals feared the camp would disperse, and that they would miss their one opportunity to deal a killing blow to Sitting Bull's resistance. On the evening of 24th June, Custer's Crow scouts brought news that the camp trail was headed west toward the Little Bighorn. This, he surmised was their only chance, a gambit worth taking, though support was too far behind him to catch up. Custer was forced – or blindly elected, depending on your interpretation of events; the jury is still out – to charge on an enemy that far outnumbered him. The battle was over before it had even begun.

After Custer's devastating defeat, the wrath of US government rained down upon the Sioux and the Cheyenne. Indians were disarmed at gunpoint as they returned to reservation agencies, including those who had taken no part in the conflict. The Black Hills were forcibly sold. Troops made attacks on tipi villages, driving any Natives who still refused to be penned in reservations into ever more precarious circumstances. Sitting Bull fled to Canada, but within a year Crazy Horse had no choice but to surrender his entourage at the Red Cloud Agency in Nebraska. A few months later and he was dead, murdered by a camp guard while purportedly resisting arrest.

It would be another four years until Sitting Bull threw down his own weapons at Fort Buford in July 1881, the last man of his tribe to surrender. He too was killed in custody while Indian agency police attempted to arrest him, fearing a potential Lakota rebellion. In almost every photographic portrait of him, Sitting Bull faces us head on, his face proud but weathered;

price guide inside back cover

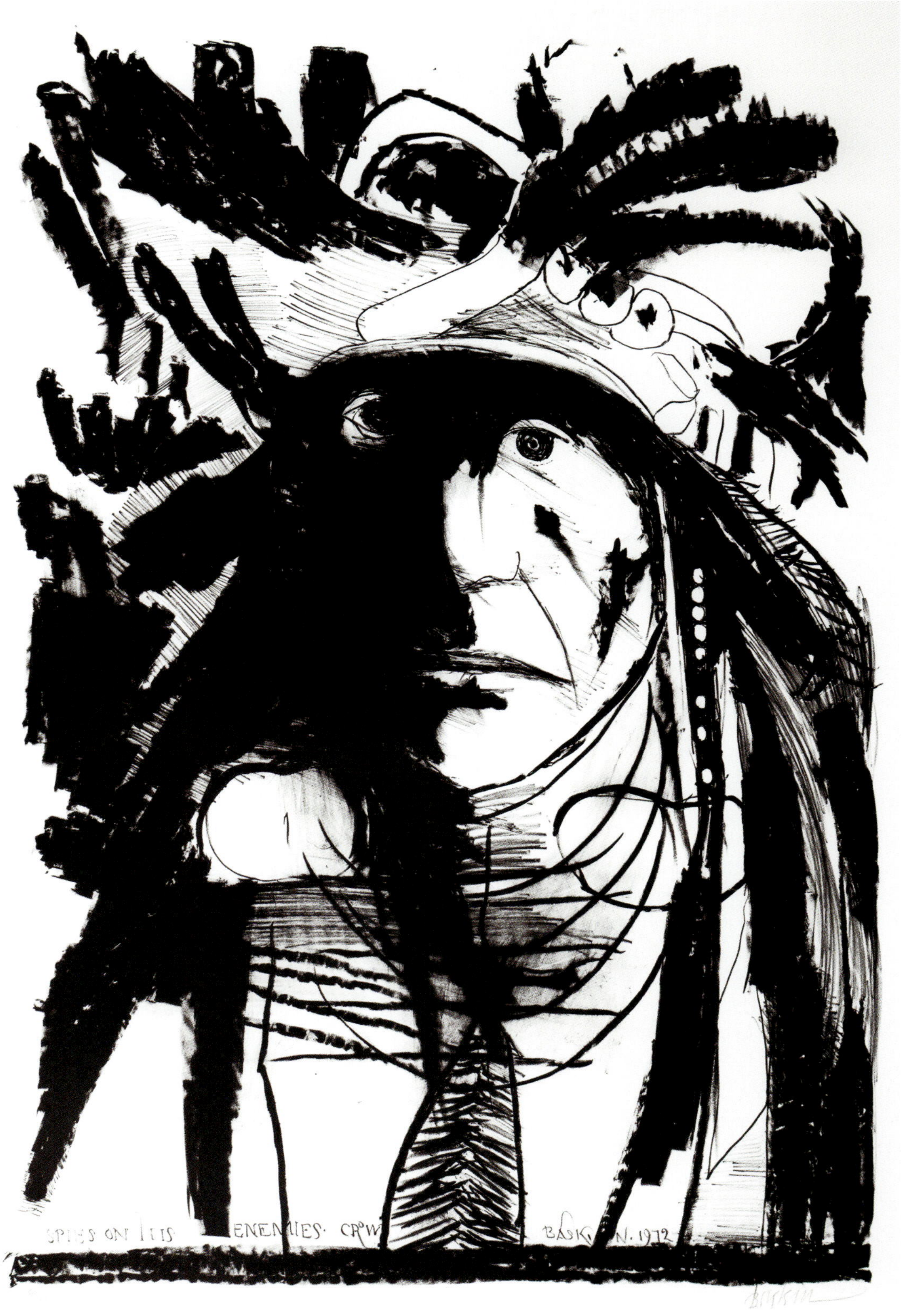

Spies on his Enemies, Crow

Baskin drew this bust after a photograph from Frank A. Rinehart's series of portraits made at the 1898 Indian Congress, which took place at the Trans-Mississippi and International Exposition, a huge world's fair. Rinehart's extensive series documented the 35 or more individual tribes who took part in the Congress, numbering more than 500 Native Americans – the largest of its kind at the time.

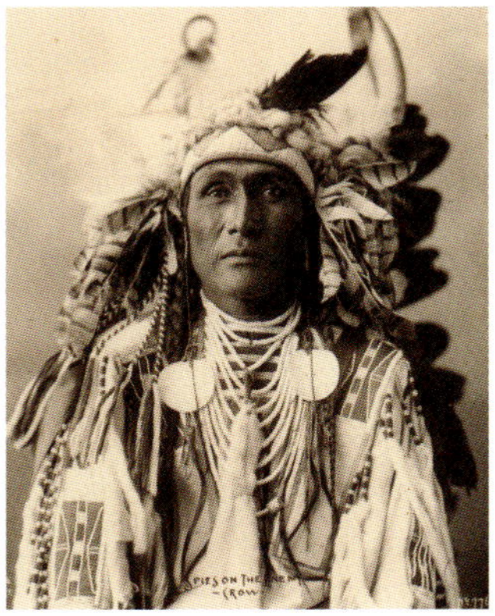

Pedro Cajete, Pueblo

Known to many in later years as 'Chief Manitou', Pedro Cajete was a member of the Pueblo Tewa tribe, near Santa Fe, New Mexico. Along with many other poor Pueblo men, his services were later hired by the sham Manitou Cliff Dwellings Museum, where he would make a living posing with tourists in a stereotypical headdress and beaded blanket.

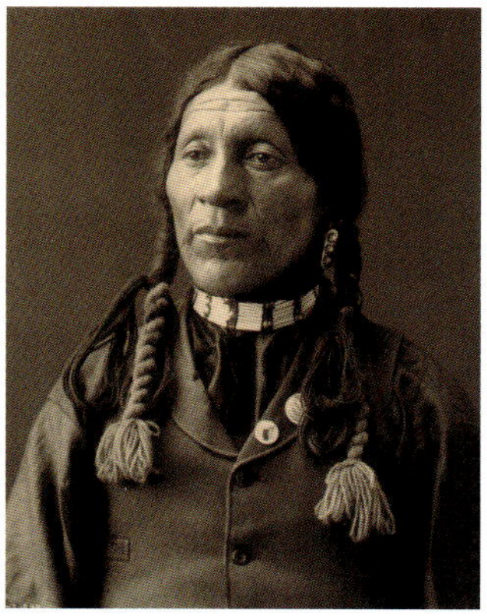

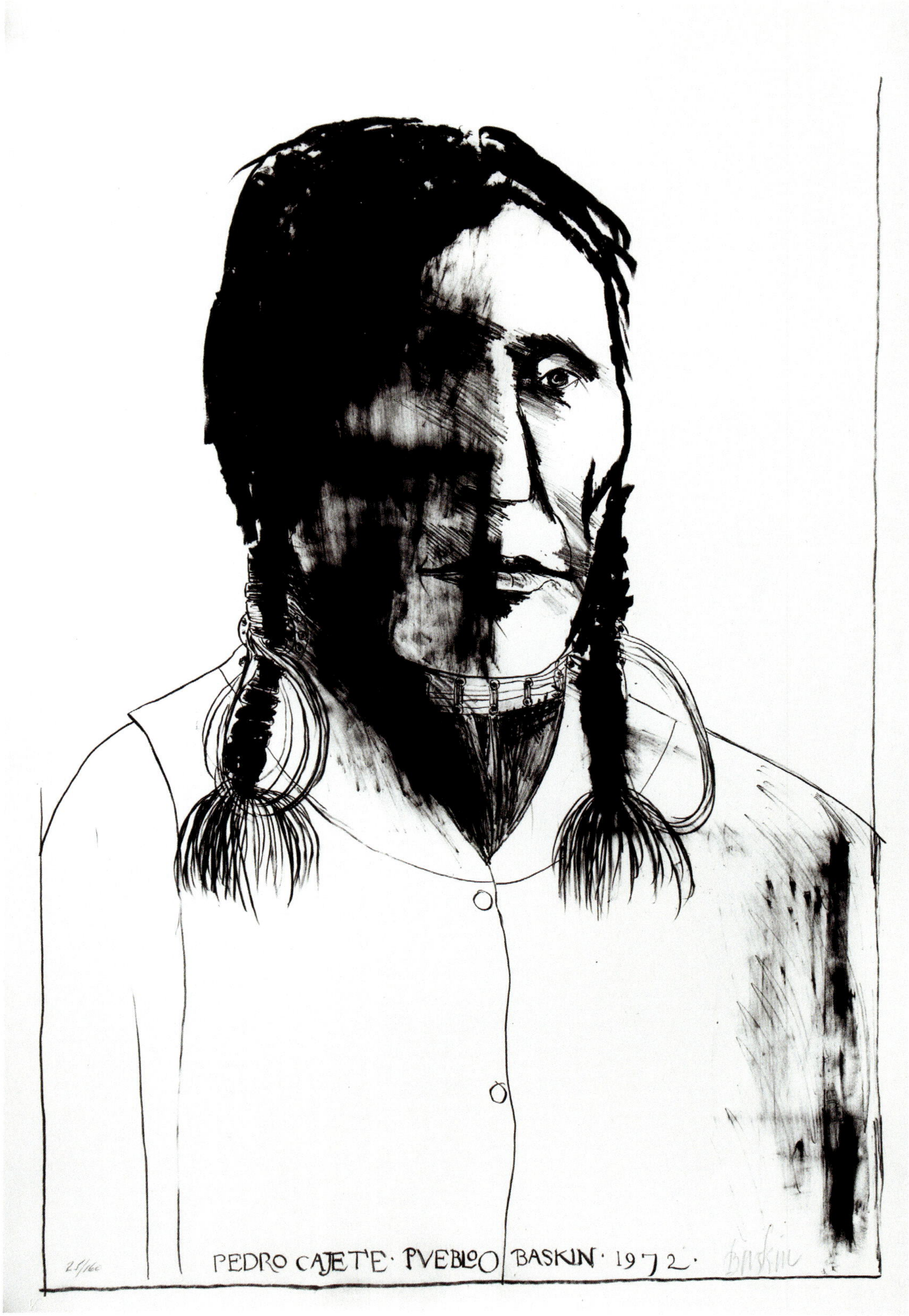

Baskin's side profile falls somewhere between Piero della Francesca's Duke and Duchess of Urbino and a police mugshot. Days later, a detachment of the 7th Cavalry (now under new management) were tasked with disarming the remaining Lakota at the agency when a gunfight turned into a massacre. As many as 300 Lakota men, women and children lay dead at the temporary camp at Wounded Knee Creek, their bodies left to freeze in the December snows.

The subjugation of Sitting Bull and Crazy Horse, representing the freedom of pre-colonial Plains life, served only to reinforce the idea of 'Manifest Destiny' prevalent among the settlers: the puritanical belief that God's designs for America had fated their expansion in the West, ever since the first Europeans had arrived. Native tribes were an obstacle to civilised progress; their destiny, by contrast, belonged to a doomed and 'primitive' past. The message now was clearer than ever: assimilate, or face extinction.

Frank A. Rinehart and Edward S. Curtis were among the more prominent photographers who attempted to document the passing of this way of life, and Baskin drew heavily, often literally, from their work. Rinehart's otherwise sympathetic portrait series of representatives from the 1898 Indian Congress in Omaha, Nebraska, contrasted the regalia of warrior headdresses against painted backgrounds and vignettes of modern living, as if to accentuate that the Indians belonged to a race confined to a bygone era. Edward Curtis, on the other hand, took a more direct approach. With a generous sponsorship from the financier J.P. Morgan, he took equipment with him as he travelled the country, living alongside the tribes he met and photographed, declaring that with his series of portraits 'I want to make them live forever.' (Among his given names were 'Shadow Catcher', in reference to his camera, and 'The Man Who Sleeps on His Breath', after the inflatable mattress on which he slept).

As beautifully captured as they are, Curtis' portraits are not perfect: he was guilty of 'dressing up' Natives in clothing they had long since abandoned, and of staging ritual performances. But they intended to preserve a dignity and reflect a stoicism that seemed fundamental to Indian survival into the early 20th century.

In 1969, as Baskin's illustrations were being put through the press, Vine Deloria Jr., a member of the Standing Rock Sioux, published the short manifesto *Custer Died for Your Sins* (the title soon caught on as a rallying cry for the American Indian movement). More than simply a call for more federal aid or political representation, in his book Deloria made the point that for too long Native Americans had existed in a monolithic state of black and white: cast as villains and heroes, noble savages tied up with a Romanticised vision of the untouched American frontier. What he yearned for was a richer understanding of the Indian identity: one that placed front and centre their sense of civic belonging, their often wryly surreal sense of humour, born of a diverse spirituality.

Leonard Baskin could find little humour in the events he was asked to portray, the people he depicted. But there are no heroic horse-back portraits, no contemporising backdrops, no egregious centring of stock Native American paraphernalia –

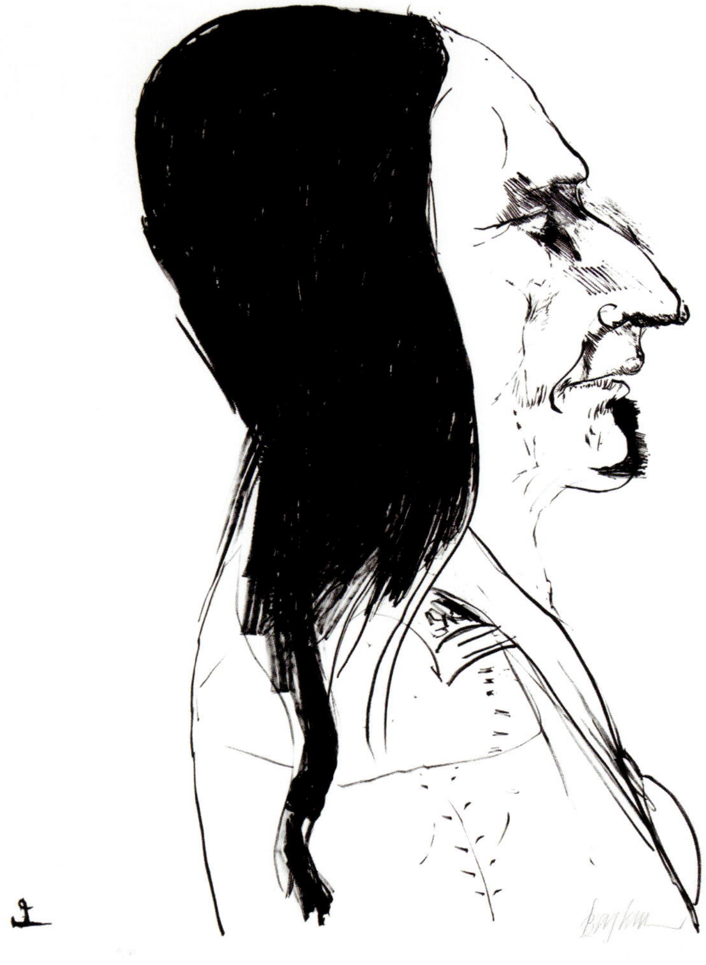

feathered headdresses, tomahawks and peace pipes – in his portraits. Instead, Mitchell Wilder writes, Baskin brings these historical figures to us – with all their cautions, their mistrust, their beauty and their melancholy – as he could, '[cutting] through a century of mediocre, apocryphal pictures to reveal the actors of this tragic drama as they were, not in the event, but in life and in death.'

Above: *Sitting Bull*, lithograph, 1972

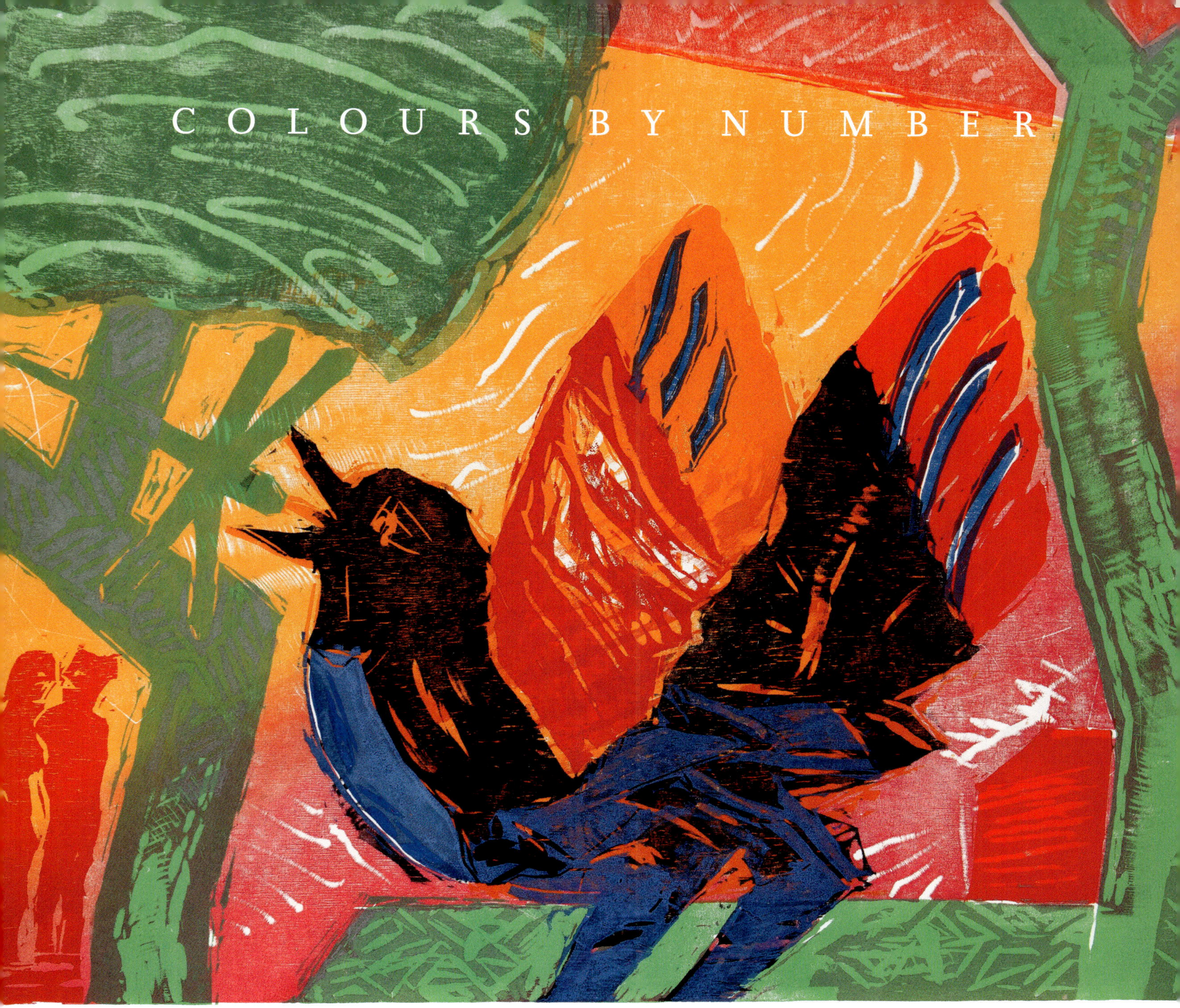

Rothenstein's Red

How the artist's childhood drawings held the key to a life-long love of vibrant vermilion

A World of Joyful Violence

Michael Rothenstein was just four years old when his father, William – then an acclaimed painter and portraitist – removed his family of six from Hampstead to an austere farmhouse in the Stroud Valley. Surrounded by the sights, sounds and smells of a new world, Rothenstein – an ambitious artist-to-be – came armed with the appropriate tools to capture these foundational images and experiences: boxes of cedar pencils, sharpened to a spear-point; stubby wax crayons in dog-eared paper jackets; chalks ground to pinchable nubs. French pastels could be crumbled between finger and thumb, like pigment smeared straight onto the page. But it was the muddying of fresh watercolour paints that revealed to him the endless possibilities of colour: 'curious grubby red and violet browns, dirty green, contrasted perhaps, with a single scream of pink or flame… I had a large tin of artists' colours which, once moistened, were invitingly juicy; most of all the brilliant warm ones, orange, cadmium yellow, and vermilion.'

There was no shortage of inspiration to be found in the objects of his father's collection, bringing colour to the walls of the otherwise spartan house. A series of Indian miniatures, amassed on Rothenstein senior's recent travels, particularly affected him, as he later recalled with the critic Mel Gooding: 'It was this element of violence, strange and dramatic happenings, in this tiny world of the miniature, and always in these very violent colours – black hills, gods and goddesses with purple and deep scarlet faces and arms, extraordinary birds flitting in and out of branches of black trees, laden with orange fruit.'

He soon found that in his own drawings, inanimate toy soldiers, engaged in silent, static battles, could be brought vividly to life. This was, as he remembered it, a full body activity. Guttural, automatic sounds accompanied frantic scribbling – 'A lot of growling and crouching when you drew lions: the noise of jabs and slashes, with ouches of pain, when you were doing battle scenes.' But most of all, his abiding memory was of that vermilion paint that gave life to his fierce and boyish imagination:

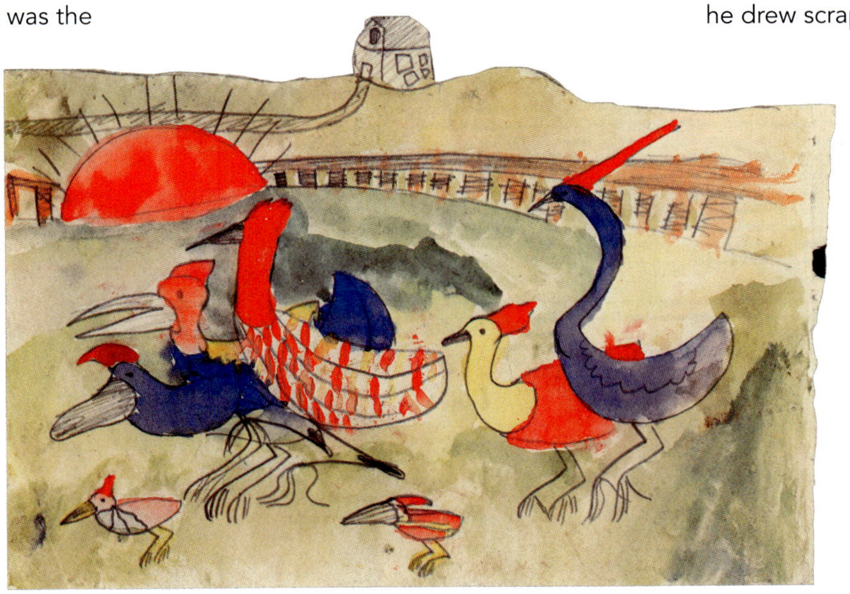

'At the battle-scene phase I needed so much red, for blood – in splashes, drips and pools – that this colour was always used up first in the paint box… Whether drawing a snapping fish, or a Saracen whirling a sabre, I illustrated a world full of violence. The severed limbs are done with cruel exuberance, joyful cruelty. Yet no childhood was ever more untroubled or closer to the arm of affection. My father continually appreciated my efforts and my mother took pleasure in preserving them. This situation fostered a wild exuberance in the face of nature and helped to concentrate feeling on the tiny privacies of an enclosed and peaceful life.'

In this very fervent imagination, the symbols and the psychology of the outside world soon cross-fertilised with private play. The plumage of tin soldier's helmets and their blazoned shields began to resemble the ornate peacockery of birds native and more exotic. Green demons with bloodied scimitars and whirling 'Red' Indians – inspired by a Native American costume gifted to his older brother, John, replete with feathered headdress and corded tassels – he drew scrapping with Tommies and Teutons. Knights held a particular mystique, 'screwed up inside steel plates' like the carapaced beetles and caddis-worms he admired by the banks of a nearby river.

Meanwhile, hundreds of miles away, his father, William, painting the ruins at Ypres, was faced with the realities of war firsthand. In his own pictures of abandoned buildings, attenuated reds, pinks and brickish browns suggested the invisible human cost behind the scenes before him. 'Over a battlefield,' he wrote, 'where the hopes and fears and passions of thousands of men were concentrated, a strange atmosphere of awe seems to hang. Throughout the desolation of war there is a pattern of austere beauty, and the human drama associated with war gives to this beauty a religious character … I felt as a pilgrim visiting sacred sites.'

In his son's hands, red was swiftly

Left: *The Garden II*, woodcut, 1990
Above: Childhood pencil drawing with watercolour, c.1912-17, published in 1986 by Redstone Press

becoming at once an emblem of the terrific ripeness and fertility of his nearby environment, and an omen of alluring danger – the kind of irresistible, almost transcendent attraction that his father had felt hanging over Belgium's fields of death. Red seemed at once to warn and to seduce: the bursting tautness of a red berry (the kind your mother warned you not to eat), the wrinkled wattle and coxcomb, the robin's chest, the cautionary patterns of ladybirds and red admirals, tortoiseshells, painted ladies, made all the more virulent by contrasts of brown, blue and black (a recurrent combination in Rothenstein's later work). This uncompromising red is a colour we crave, that commands the eye: the red of bright blood on a fresh cut, the red carpet, a red rag to a bull. And this collision of violence, danger, attraction, and radiance, lies at the very red-blooded heart of Michael Rothenstein's art.

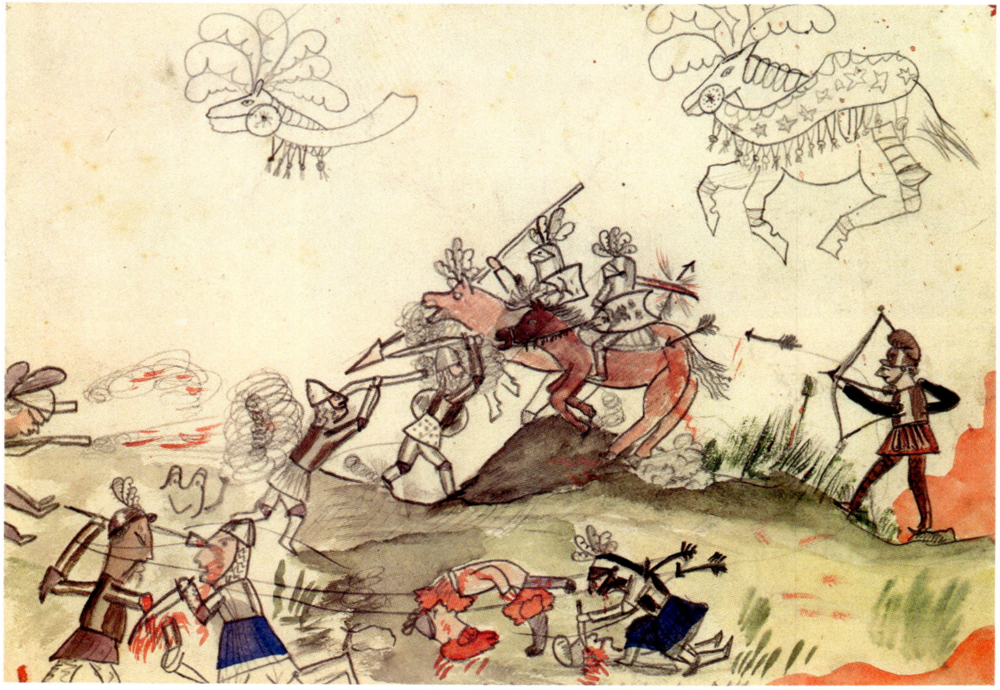

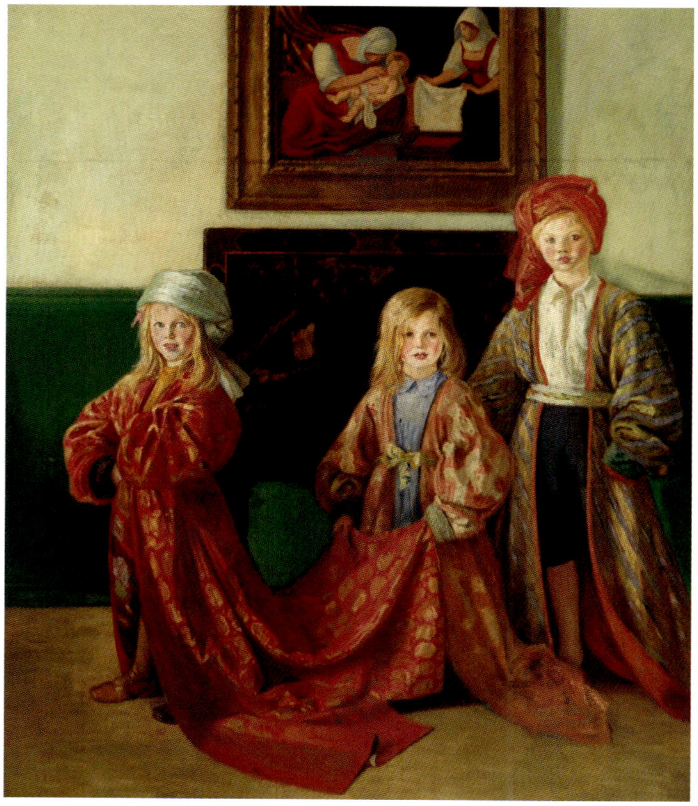

Top: Childhood pencil drawing with watercolour, c.1912-17, published in 1986 by Redstone Press

Bottom: William Rothenstein, *The Princess Badroulbadour*, 1908; Michael's elder siblings, John, Betty and Rachel, serve as models

Opposite: *Christmas Tree*, linocut, c. 1954

Red Stones

Preserved for over 70 years, Michael Rothenstein's childhood drawings were published in a large, slim booklet in 1986 by the Redstone Press. In fact it was Redstone's inaugural publication, the press founded by Julian, Michael's son, who took a straight translation of their surname as its imprint. Theirs was one of many geographical German names, locating its bearers near to one of the large, red granite or sandstone boulders that occasionally neighboured Germany's riverside towns. Some, according to local stories, were the tombs of children or princesses who had been trapped by evil witches – hence their blood-red hue.

This particular branch of the Rothenstein family had lived for centuries in Grohnde, near Hamelin, where William's Jewish forebears had kept a small but prosperous mill. Moritz, William's father, then emigrated to Bradford in the 1860s

price guide inside back cover

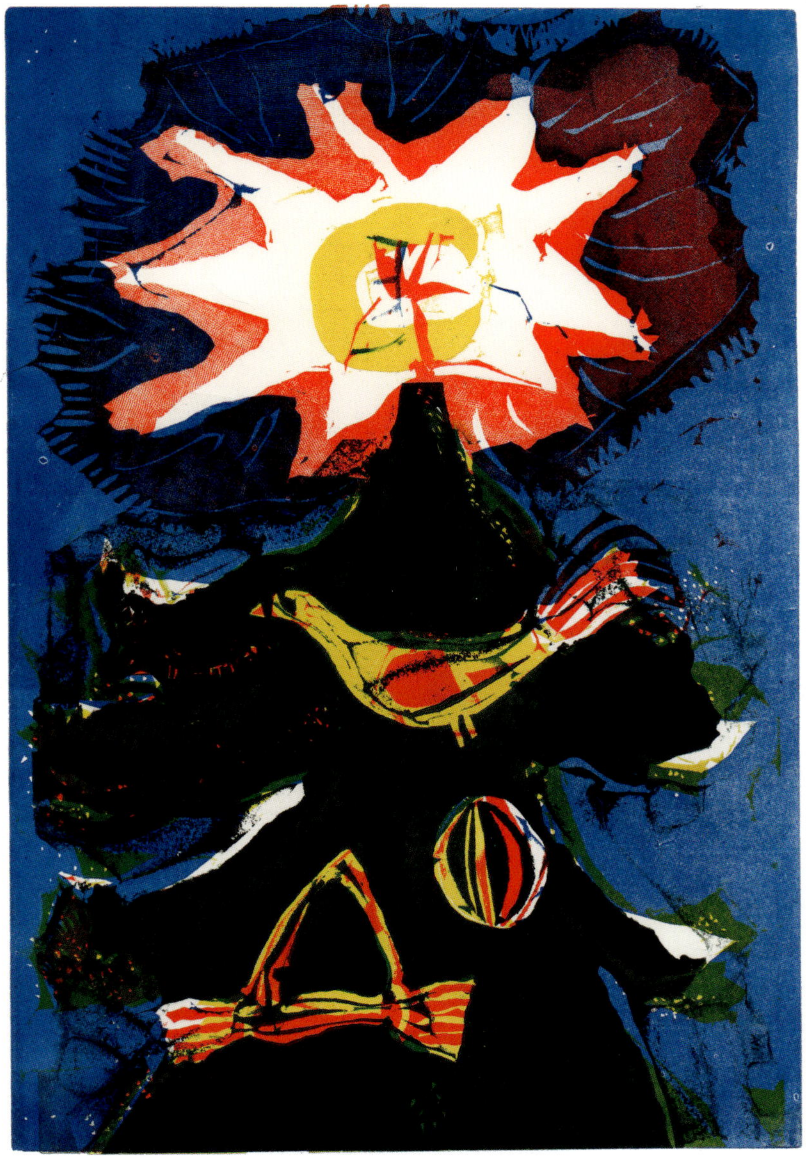

to further his fortunes in the woollen trade, preserving his devout wife's Hungarian-Jewish heritage under the protection of the Unitarian church. As a young boy, William fell under the spell of a local pastor before leaving to become an artist, training first at the Slade, then in the Montmartre garrets of Paris. His friend, the writer Max Beerbohm, described the prim and slightly self-serious painter who emerged from his Parisian apprenticeship as a 'Japanese Jew with a Franco-German accent. He *was* foreign.' And so his four children (of whom Michael was the youngest) grew up in a cultured home that blended Jewish intimacy, fraternity and good humour with an Anglo-Catholic love of things, relics, ritual. Christmases were thoroughly Germanic: William describes in one letter 'a very harlequinade of a tree' dominating the dining room, 'with blue and red balls, and fairy dolls and monkey up-sticks and glass birds playing hide and seek with one another among the branches.' For the impressionable young Michael here lay another pivotal childhood memory: an image of the outside world brought into the privacy of the home, profound, above all, in its outpouring of colour and light:

'I was simply blinded with joy. It seemed to me so beautiful, so perfectly fulfilling, an image of endless, endless happiness, and endless joy. And that idea, that concept of lights, gleaming in darkness, has really resonated through all my experience of the outside world…Of fairgrounds, the idea of coloured lights, shining out of darkness, is related to a great deal that I found very, very moving. Not only the first things you think of, the moon, or a cluster of stars, but there's something very touching about a beckoning light. A moment of human truthfulness, shining in the darkness...'

Blood and Soil

In 1920, the same year William was appointed Director of the Royal College of Art, the family sold Iles Farm, moving back to Campden Hill, Kensington. But the non-conformity of his countryside upbringing had already made a lasting impression on Michael, intent now on a career in art but with a very different vision of what that meant from his father's cosmopolitan circle.

The young man who William now began to introduce to artist friends seemed 'Franciscan, Tolstoyan, collarless and lean, ashamed of our possessions and of our conventionalities.' He was impressed by a studio visit to Stanley Spencer, who described how his own 'earthly paradise' had been shattered by the war and he now found himself piecing it back together again. But it was a meeting with the printmaker Barnett Freedman that introduced him to the inspiring 'proletariat' world of printmaking, leagues

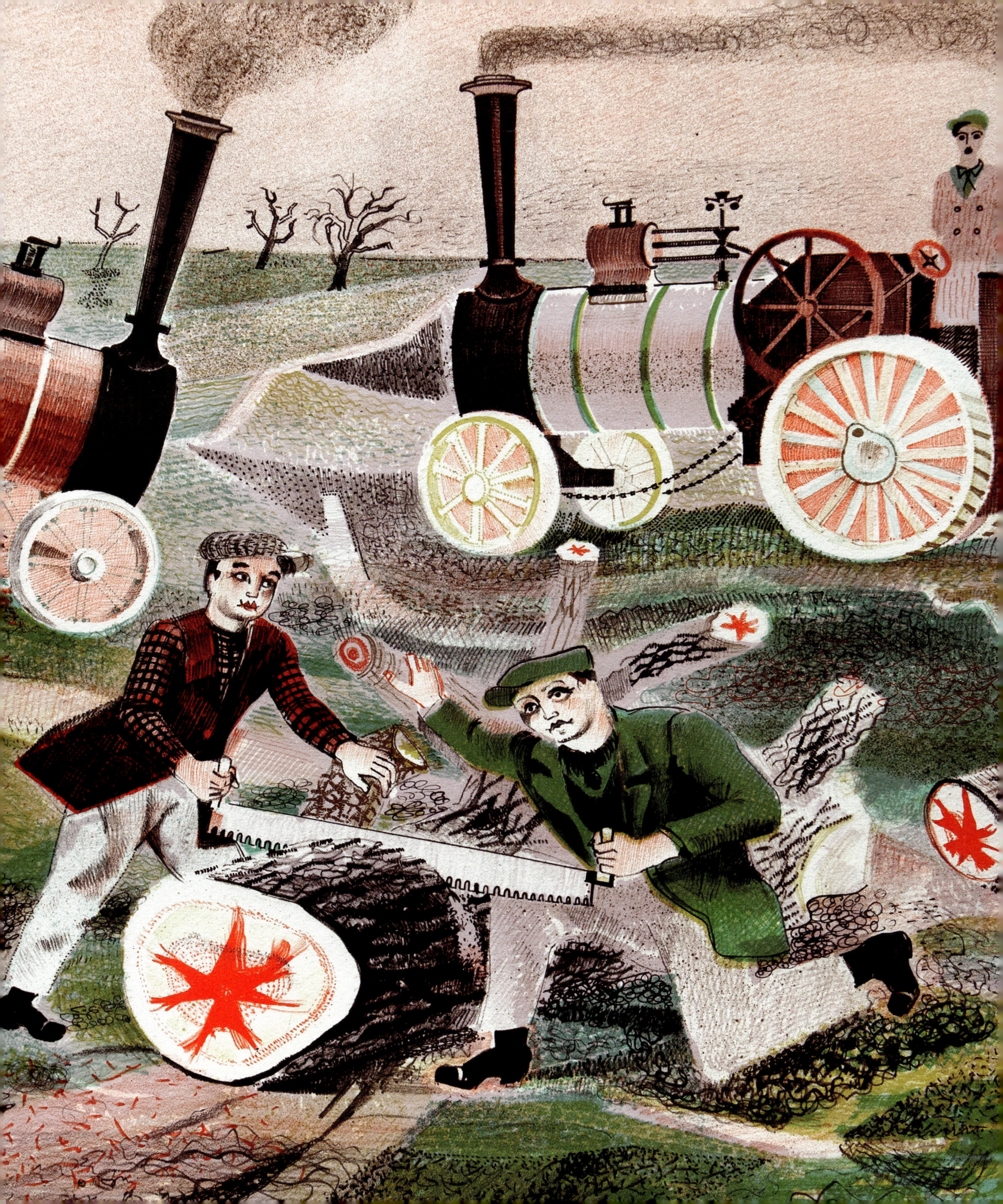

apart from the high-society milieu of which his father and mother were then a part. Freedman, then practising at a Working Men's College in Mornington Crescent, kept a studio filled with the kind of hard-edged, mechanical paraphernalia – among them architectural designs and heaps of photographs – that represented the 'wonderful slummy London' Michael yearned to explore.

But in 1926 he was stopped in his tracks, struck down with myxoedema, a hypothyroid condition that gripped him for another 16 years. His doctor advised that he should not draw: 'his imagination is so stirred at present that it plays him tricks.' And though he felt little pain, the illness brought with it instead feelings of intense, prolonged, near-suicidal dread, a double, shadowed vision, and raging fear. 'If I was left, when I was in bad shape, in a room with a carving knife,' he told Gooding, 'I would be completely obsessed by it, either to cut my own throat, or the throat of anybody else in the room. It was so terrible.'

Without the energy to drive his own art forward, he turned instead to criticism of others. 'He analyses my paintings,' his father wrote to Beerbohm in September, 1934: 'psycho-analyses me, challenges, cites, collates, chides, and corrects any constructive looseness he discovers. His mind has become a formidable one; and as he can imitate anyone, speech, gesture, accent manner, so, without books, he appears to grasp ideas. He overtops me in height, and in everything else.'

For several years, Michael Rothenstein had illustrated his own imaginary battles while his father sought to establish the role of the Official War Artist at the Western Front. Now, two decades later, came a cruel irony. Near Grohnde, past the banks of the Weser up Bückeburg hill, Nazi officials marshalled the local farmers attending 'Das Reichserntedankfest' – a vast festival celebrating the 'blood and soil' of the German people. This rural pageantry represented the largest of any Nazi gathering, bigger even than the Nuremberg rallies. Wehrmacht troops performed in mock skirmishes, replete with soldiery, panzers and passing bomber planes. In displays of martial and agricultural superiority, the festival promoted the Aryan ideology of a pure-bred race on native ground – trampling over the multicultural past from which the Rothenstein family had emerged.

Red Essex

As his health began to return, Michael Rothenstein sought the countryside once more. From a family cottage in Far Oakridge, Stroud, he moved in 1941 to the artists' commune at Great Bardfield. In the decade before, Essex itself had turned red. Five miles west of Bardfield, Conrad Noel – known as the 'Red Vicar' – presided over the parish in Thaxted, preaching a Christian socialist message that had begun to spread throughout the county. His determination to hang the red flag alongside the Irish tricolour and the cross of St George prompted a much-publicised feud with Cambridge students, who would steal the offending items in scuffles with Noel known as the 'battle of the flags'.

More broadly, the colour red had infiltrated other corners of the rural world. Rothenstein had described how the black and white geometry of the farmyard – of wooden constructions, outhouses and fences, tarred and white-washed – had made a forceful impression on his childhood art. Now a more violent irruption was occurring in fields across the country as farming of a completely different kind, bolstered by industry and new mechanical machinery, took place. Several miles away, in deepest Essex, British Ford established their headquarters and factory lines. New petrol tractors, with their distinct red cast iron wheels, could be easily spotted on the horizon of ploughed fields. Two make their appearance in Rothenstein's 1947 School Print, *Timber Felling*, operated by a gang of Stakhanovite workers, the red-star heart of dismembered logs echoing the wheels of the machines behind them.

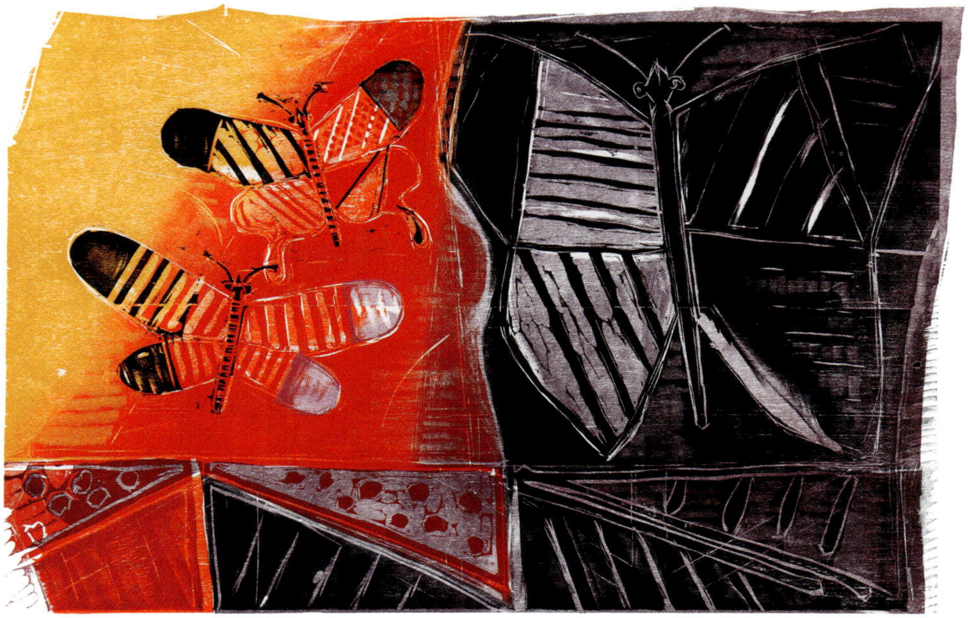

Opposite *Timber Felling*, School Print series, lithograph, 1946
Above: *Butterflies I*, woodcut, 1982

William Rothenstein did not see the end of the Second World War, dying in February 1945. Nor did he witness the extraordinary, chrysalis-like transformation of his youngest son's art, from Neo-Romantic painter to experimental printmaker; from Cezanne-esque oil and watercolour landscapes to rich, coarse

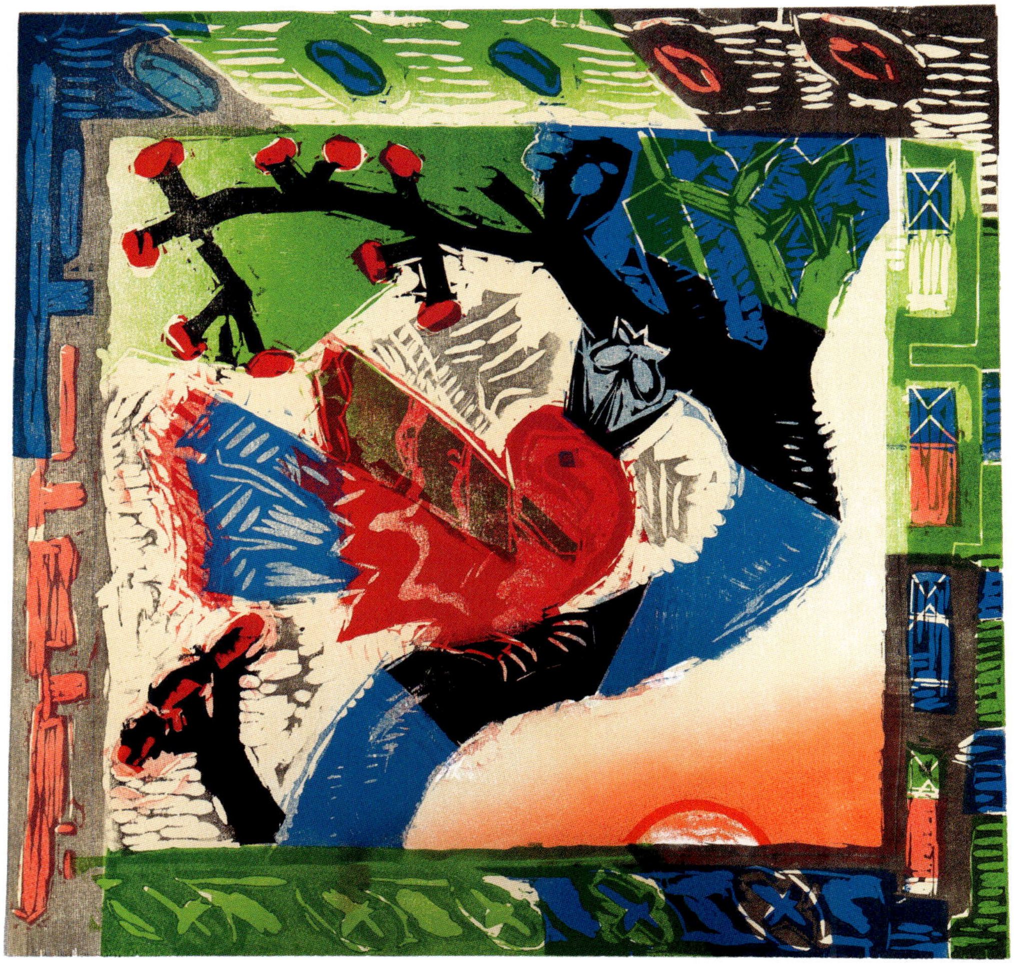

descriptions of rural life, in all its fantastically ugly splendour; owls and turkeys and berry-bearing trees, in wood and linoleum cuts, to a growing abstract symbology, an embrace of photographic material and cultural refuse, to screenprinting's capacity for immediate analogy and juxtaposition – a merry-go-round of exploratory technique-busting and metamorphing subject matter over forty years.

His love of this vibrant cadmium red remained at the heart of this work. But from the early 1980s especially, in the last decade of Rothenstein's life, he made a specific return to those early childhood drawings which continued to resonate, seven decades later. He was then living in Stisted, his work caught between urban and rural scenes: Blakeian underworlds – dive cafes and tube station dioramas – and the lost Eden of the country backyard, where flourished his recognisably exotic birds. Most were woodcuts, and all were cut with a very un-urbane urgency and nerve, a compressed energy, like the grain of the wood itself, which he called its 'graph of energy', pressed tight and thick in on itself and threatening to split. As Mel Gooding pointed out, there were deep, psychic correspondences between his method and the worlds he depicted: the way a city grows outward, for example, like the rings of a tree trunk, or how a split in the grain might mirror a river carving through the city.

Colours collide and splash like fireworks in these late prints: red crashes into orange, violet, yellow, green. Many involved Romanesque borders that required a complex jig-sawing of multiple blocks of wood, colours overlapping like light scattered through stained glass. Ann Westley and then Anna Elinson worked as assistants in these later years, printing on the Columbian press that is now housed in the Goldmark Atelier, under the aegis of its crimson eagle counterweight. A frequent refrain, among the remembrances of all his studio hands, was of Rothenstein's creative impulsiveness, his impatience with the technical side of things, his untameable desire to change, alter, jump in at any moment – an utterly un-repetitive approach to a medium that was supposed to embody routine, embracing mistakes at every turn.

At the heart of it lay a fascination with the violent fertility of the natural world – 'a pleasurable reverence', as he later put it, 'in co-operating with an object that was in fact torn from the very heart of nature.' The critic Peter Fuller put it even more simply: 'Those butterflies and birds, of the new woodcuts – they have flown out of the Paradise of your infancy.'

Above left: *Red Berries*, woodcut, 1992
Opposite: Michael Rothenstein, *Roman Zoo*, woodcut, 1986

HIGHLIGHTS

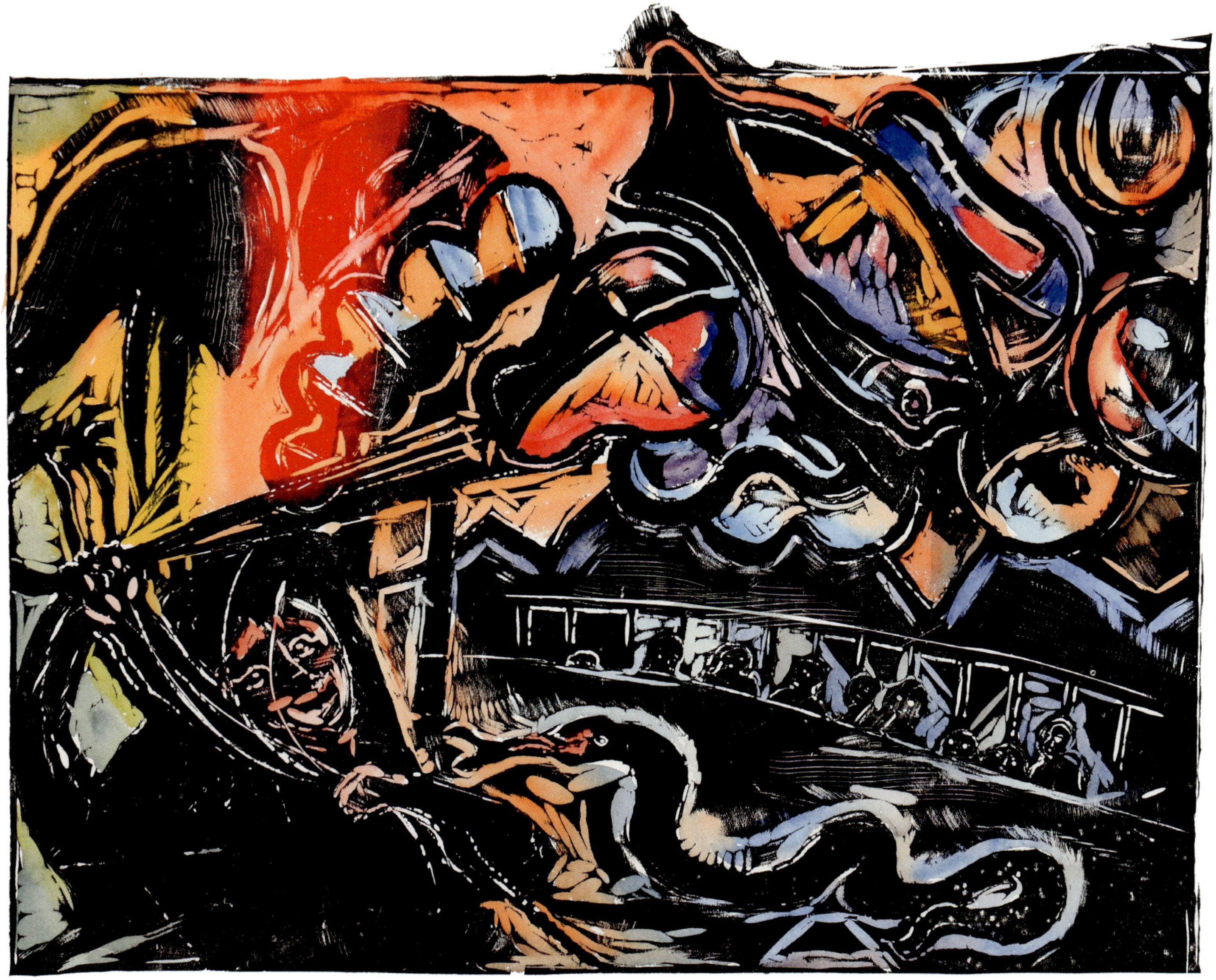

Curator **Julian Spalding** illuminates the art of **Francis Davison**, writer **Mark Haddon** is nourished by the pots of **Jean-Nicolas Gérard**, and a suite of rare **Picasso** woodcuts joins new arrivals at the gallery

New To The Gallery

Our latest art and ceramics arrivals

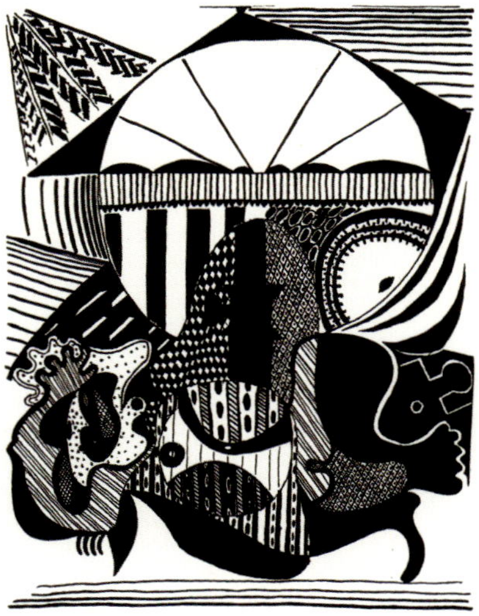

Pablo Picasso, *Hélène Chez Archimède*

Having handled the full breadth of Picasso's graphic work here at the gallery, this is the very first time we have come across this particular set of woodcuts, engraved by the artist Georges Aubert after Picasso's designs which he made in 1925 to illustrate a play by André Suarès. Originally commissioned by the great publisher Ambroise Vollard, the suite was one of many projects that remained unfinished on Vollard's sudden death in 1939. In 1955 it was finally resurrected by a Parisian publisher. Printed in an overall edition of 240, those illustrated here are from a special edition of just 100. A remarkable opportunity to own a print deriving from a fascinating period of Picasso's life, available only by the delay in the project.

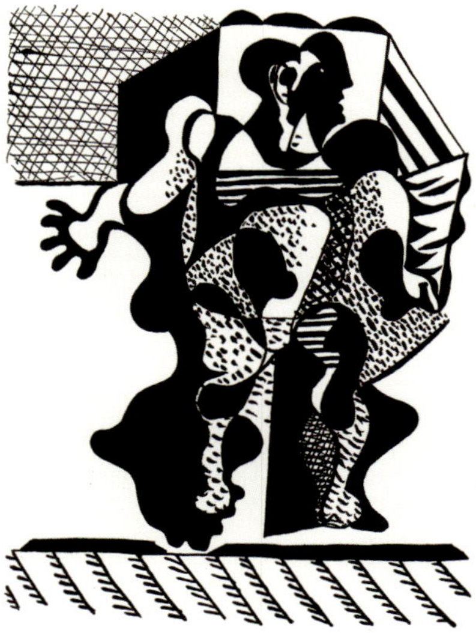

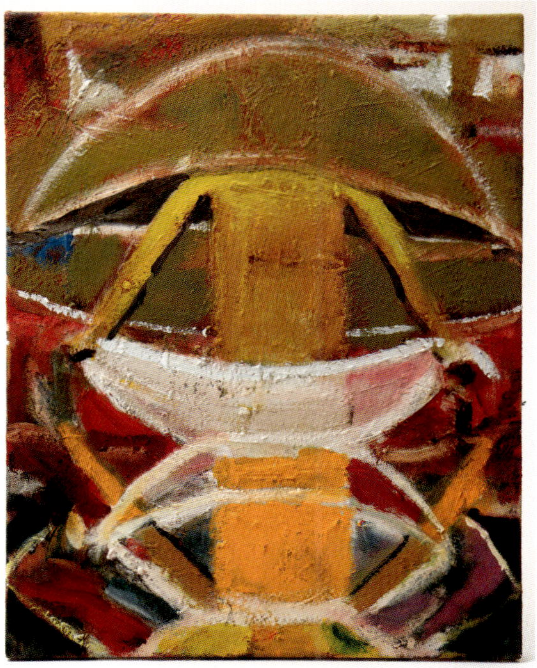

Oliver Bancroft, *Umbrellas*

'The paintings of Oliver Bancroft have such immediacy, such presence,' writes Iain Sinclair, 'that they defy rational explanation.' In the last few years Bancroft has returned to his enigmatic ways with paint, producing pictures that shore up their inner mysteries against a sense of familiarity. This unknown figure, reflected waist-high in a pool of water: have we seen him before somewhere? Golden bathers standing in cauldrons or stripped at the beach, reminiscent of della Francesca's *Baptism of Christ*, are a recurring motif in Bancroft's work – but their significance remains as elusive as ever.

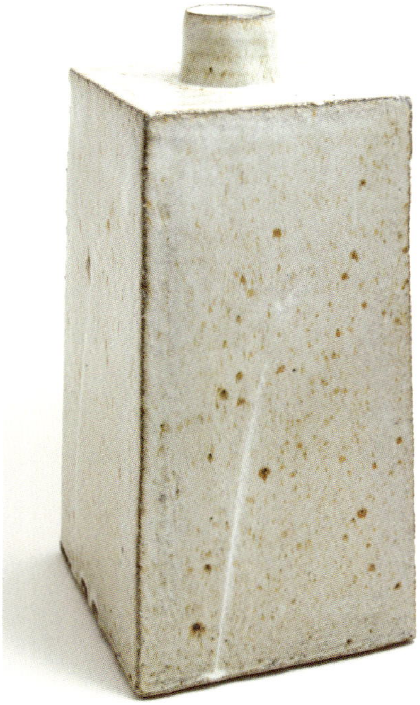

Anne Mette Hjortshøj, *Oblong Press-Moulded Bottle*

Life has not got any slower for Danish potter Anne Mette Hjortshøj. Her Wild Clay project, established to rediscover the natural clay deposits dotted about the island of Bornholm, has picked up plenty of steam, expanding her already impressive repertoire of clays, slips and glazes. The inlaid porcelain grass motif on this bottle offers a beautiful evocation of the island landscape itself.

Most of the items featured in this magazine are available for purchase. Phone us for a chat on 01572 821424 or see more and buy online at goldmarkart.com

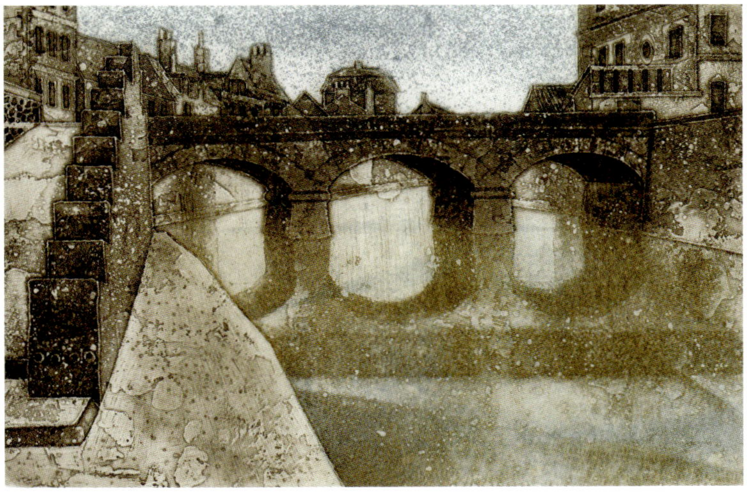

Valerie Thornton, *The Loire at Vendôme*

Valerie Thornton (1931-91) remains something of an unsung figure in 20th century British printmaking. Though she kept herself to predominantly topographical subject matter in her prints – with a special emphasis on weathered architectural details – her extraordinary talents in etching and aquatint were honed with the most avant-garde printmakers of the 1950s and '60s, studying at Stanley Hayter's Atelier 17 and spending two years in New Yorkat the Pratt Institute. This delightfully textured etching is a case in point.

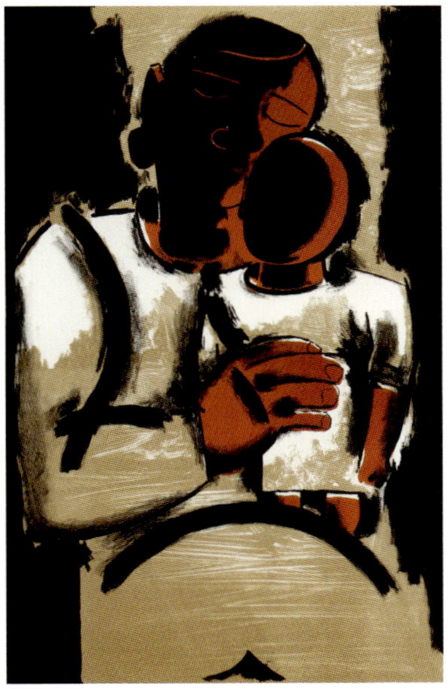

Josef Herman, *Mother and Child*

Josef Herman (1911-2000) was one of many young Jewish emigrés who sought safety in the UK with the rise of Nazi Germany, arriving in Glasgow by way of the Polish Air Force. Though best known for his depictions of the Welsh mining community he called home for 11 years, this tender domestic scene was made on his return to London, soon after his marriage to his wife, Nini, mother of their three children.

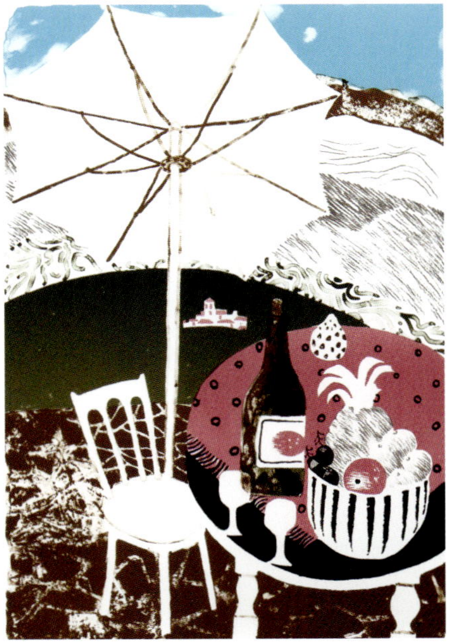

Mary Fedden, *Picnic*

Mary Fedden (1915-2012) joins a still growing list of British artists intent on exploring the endlessly adaptable traditions of the still life. As a student at the Slade, she worked under the theatre designer Vladimir Polunin, Sergei Diaghilev's favoured scene-painter, instilling a fascination with the theatre that informed her later work too: in this lithograph, textures, colours and white-space shapes are collaged like stage props for a peopleless scene.

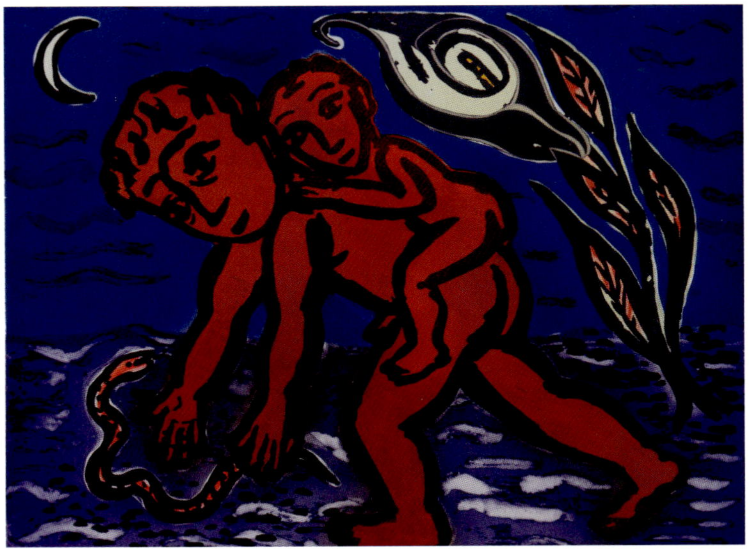

Eileen Cooper, *The Lesson*

Eileen Cooper has forged a career with the dreamlike and deceivingly naive figuration for which she is now celebrated. *The Lesson* joins five other large etchings new to the gallery, made some 25 years ago at the Radical Print Centre when Cooper was still lecturing at the Royal College of Art. She was later made Head of Printmaking at the Royal Academy and in 2011 became the Academy's first woman to hold the title of Keeper. Head to our website for a very special offer on these six prints.

Jean-Nicolas Gérard: Unrestrained Celebration

Mark Haddon on the 'joyous rightness' of a favourite French potter

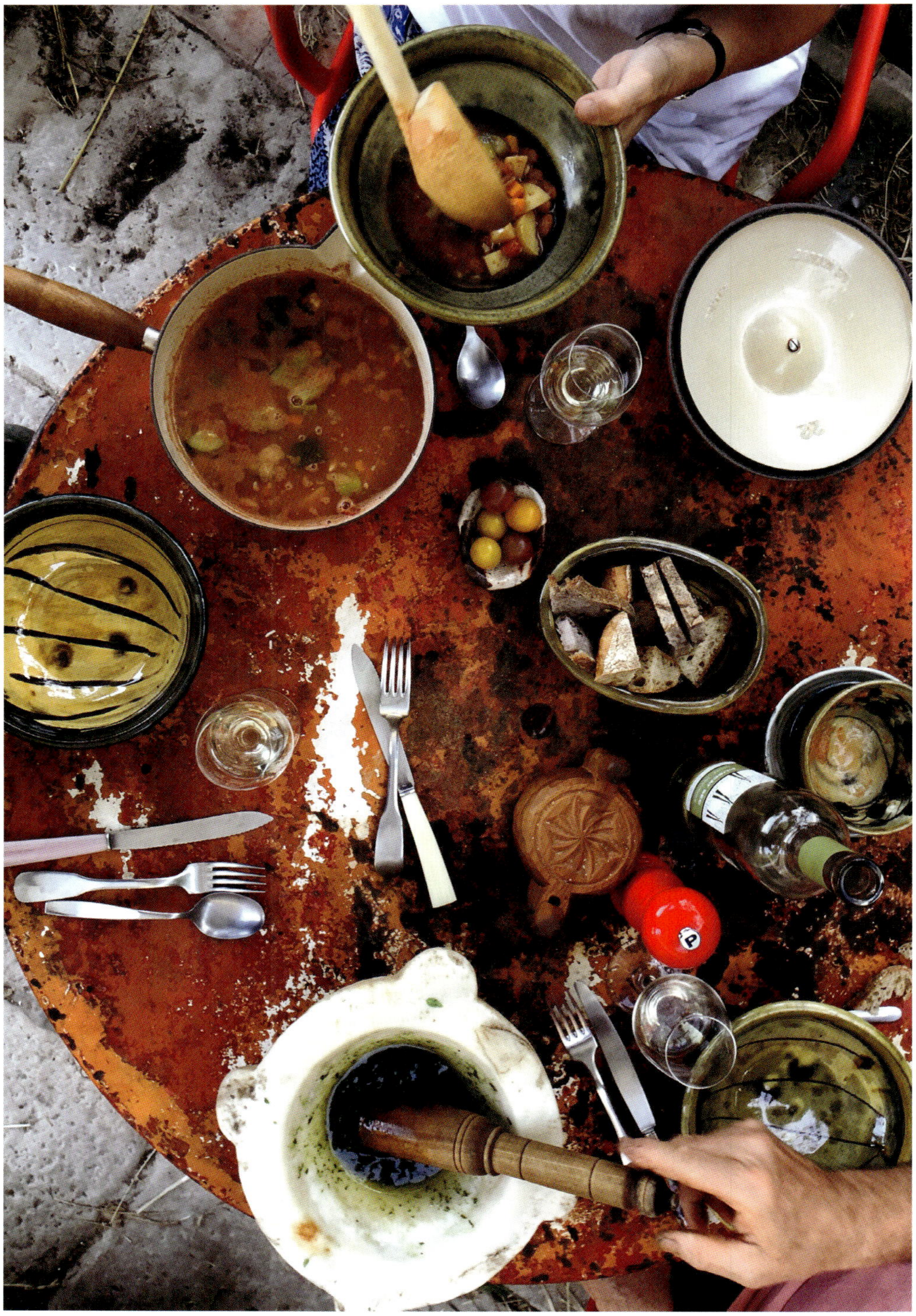

I first found myself on the Goldmark website some years ago in search of prints from David Hockney's *Grimm's Fairy Tale* series. I had little or no interest in ceramics at the time. My favourite mug was a gift from Thamesmead Prison where I'd done a workshop, printed with an aerial view of the prison and the legend 'HMP Thamesmead – Wish You Were Here'. My favourite plate was a standard store-bought item with a white centre and a custard yellow border from which I ate toast and Alphabetti Spaghetti as a child in the 1960s and which has miraculously survived for nearly 60 years. Most ceramics, for me, fell into the uncomfortable void between utensils and art objects. Perhaps I was too much of a literalist but to buy a beautiful bowl, vase or platter intending only to look at it seemed a kind of pretence, dishonest almost.

Then, to my surprise, I saw photographs of Jean-Nicolas Gérard's work and fell in love.

I find it relatively easy to say why some art fails to touch me. I find it much harder to explain why other art moves me deeply. Indeed I think that inability is often a vital part of the attraction. It takes me to a place where the words don't go. It's a puzzle which keeps asking to be solved but never quite

'Hidden sophistication be damned; looseness, roughness and spontaneity are qualities to be celebrated in and of themselves…'

gives up the answer. In consequence everything that comes below is perhaps nothing more than an attempt to post-rationalise something ineffable, the gut-reaction I feel when I look at Jean-Nicolas Gérard's work and hold it in my hands. But let me try.

One, it's made to be used. It looks that way and it feels that way. I drink my first cup of tea every day from one of his beakers and eat my muesli from one of his bowls. If you come round for lunch we'll probably be using his plates. And that's exactly what Jean-Nicolas Gérard intends. Watch the Goldmark video interview with him at his studio in Provence and look at the lunch he lays out in the garden - tomato salad, cheese, bread and aubergine caviar all presented on his plates and platters. They look beautiful doing nothing, but they look best when they're doing what they were made to do.

Two, it's loose and rough and spontaneous. Having said which, it's tempting to add, 'but this belies a hidden sophistication' or some such qualification. But you wouldn't make a similar defence of a painting by Jean-Michel Basquiat or a sculpture by Phyllida Barlow. Hidden sophistication be damned; looseness, roughness and spontaneity are qualities to be celebrated in and of them-selves when lines and shapes seem to flow from an artist's hands with this kind of joyous rightness.

Three, it's utterly transparent. Everything involved in its making is visible in the finished object – the turning, cutting, bending and moulding of the clay, the fingerprints, the splotches of an old paint brush, the scratches made in the coloured slip with a burin or a stick. Nothing is hidden. It's like watching a magician show you the secret to their trick then doing it all over again and the trick being just as magical as it was the first time.

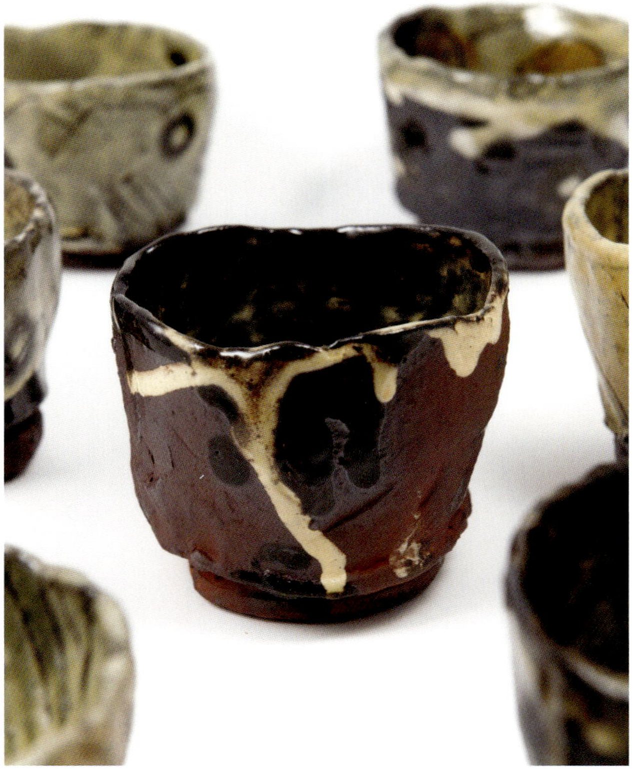

Four, it's gloriously analogue. I know it's the wrong antithesis to apply to pottery, but the digital nature of the modern world means that everywhere we are drowning in smoothness, so that I've come, more and more, to appreciate impasto, smudges, thumbprints, brush marks, anything that says, 'This was made by a human being'. The double pleasure of holding work by Jean-Nicolas is that you often find your own hand settling into dints and troughs made by his as they shaped the clay or patterned the slip. Indeed, most of the drinking vessels he makes are slightly compressed on either side by his thumb and middle finger so that they fit perfectly into your hand and you find yourself holding them just as he held them.

Five, it's joyous. If we are beset by an excess of smoothness in the wider world then we're beset by an excess of coolness in the world of contemporary art. There is a wide-spread embarrassment about big, positive emotions, as if they are naïve and childish. Far better to hide behind the ironic, the arch, the wry, the pretence of disaffection. In contrast to this way of thinking, Jean-Nicolas Gérard's work throws its arms wide and feels no embarrassment whatsoever. It is an unrestrained celebration of clay and colour, of shape and form and volume, of sitting down together round a table and eating and drinking.

There is an oft-repeated maxim that Jean-Nicolas Gérard is 'the potter's potter'. I think this does him a disservice. It suggests something narrow and arcane about his work which can properly be understood only by other practitioners who share some kind of specialised knowledge. On the contrary, I doubt there is another potter out there whose work is more easily understood and more eager to be used.

Hand-built cups, slipware, 2024

Light in the Art of Francis Davison

Julian Spalding reflects on the lifelong work of a close friend

'Now is life very solid or very shifting? I am haunted by the two contradictions. This has gone on forever: will last forever: goes down to the bottom of the world – this moment I stand on. Also, it is transitory, flying diaphanous. I shall pass like a cloud on the waves. Perhaps it may be that though we change, one flying after another, so quick, so quick, yet we are somehow successive, and continuous – we human beings: and show the light through. But what is the light?'

Virginia Woolf. Diaries. 4th January 1929

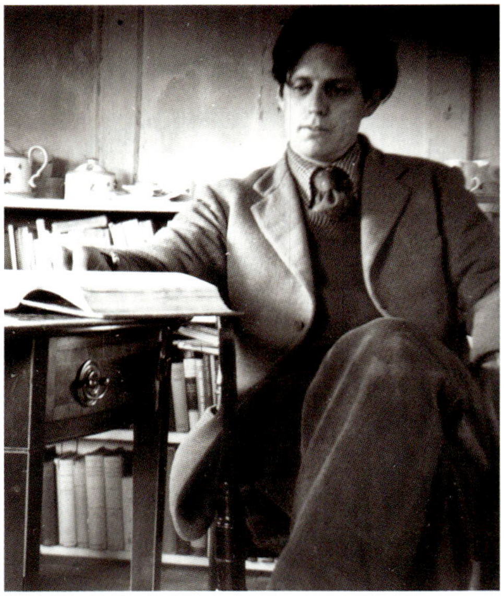

Anyone lucky enough to have a Francis Davison on their wall at home, as I do, is living with what I can only call 'the light of life'. I want to try to describe, as best I can, what this 'light' actually could be.

We need light to see and, because of that, we've tended to elide seeing with illumination, so much so that we used to think that seeing was a beam of light that came out of the eye and could physically touch what we saw. Belief in the Evil Eye and the Beneficent Eye was widespread, if not universal. It was only about four hundred years ago that scientists in Western Europe discovered how seeing actually works. They realised, ironically during the age we now call the Enlightenment, that the eye is a passive receptacle of rays and that no light comes out of it at all. As a consequence, many Christians have come to think, like their mother and sister faiths, Judaism and Islam, that the God they believe in cannot be seen. Looking has ceased to have any power on earth and anything spiritual has receded out of sight. In addition, we discovered that our eyes are limited in scope. Many things in the universe can only be seen with the aid of a microscope or telescope. Seeing with the naked eye has shrunk in significance. This has, overall, been bad news for visual art.

But this isn't the end of a story. Raymond Tallis, the neuroscientist, philosopher and polymath, thinks that something does come out of the eye even though we can't see it. Whenever anyone looks at us, we, more often than not, feel something. And these feelings can be very intense, among the most intense experiences of connection we ever have. We still tend to think of a look as a 'light' that comes out of the eye, and we tend, too, to associate this light with life, for this is the 'light' in someone's eyes that goes out when they die.

This 'light of life', we now know, isn't something physical, like a flame or a torch, not even a star, nor the one nearest to us, a sun. But it's still 'there' in a real sense. What we seem to be doing, when we look into someone else's eyes, and connect with them, is to share, for a moment, our separate consciousnesses, our individual self-awareness that we are both alive in this moment and that this moment is fleeting. We are back in Virginia Woolf's eternal present in which we can only live but which we know, too, is forever passing – and we think we can see the 'light' that radiates within this exchange.

What is extraordinary and, as far as I am aware, unique in Francis Davison's art is that he developed, over thirty years, a visual language that enabled him to play with and create this 'light', differently, distinctly and glowingly, day after day after day. But this is where this article becomes challenging – how can one describe in words a visual experience that reaches beyond sight?

Francis rarely said anything about what he was actually doing, even to me who possibly knew him better than anyone, apart from his wife, the artist, Margaret Mellis. He was not only chronically retiring; he had no patience with anyone who didn't actually see what he'd done, freshly, without trying to categorize his work in terms of, for example, the historical development of abstraction from representation. He didn't deign to explain anything, just as he didn't date, sign or title any of his works. He hardly sold anything during his life, living, very modestly, with his wife, on the income her paintings occasionally brought and by selling eggs from the many chickens he reared.

'The whole process is there, even what was cut out or what was used and discarded until something modest appears, a satisfactory balance, a stillness, a suggestive form.'

His art is about what do you do when you have nothing else to do, just live. Samuel Beckett, when asked why he wrote in French, not English, replied, 'I wanted to impoverish myself further.' Davison used the most basic materials, torn and cut, self-coloured, robust papers, used in packaging, never paint and brushes. Some of the marks on his collages look like brush-marks, and they are in the sense that they're traces of paper left on the glue he applied (with a brush) to stick his papers together, which he subsequently tore apart. Towards the end he cannibalized old works to make new ones. That's one reason why so much of his work is impossible to date; each piece is often the product of accumulated feeling and thinking over years.

'A mess taking shape until something modest appears' sums up his working method. What is exceptional about his work is that, while it remains a mess – he never smoothed anything out, or tidied up a corner or a tear – and yet it always resonates. Every fleck, every nick in Davison's work is always meant. Nothing ends being left to chance, yet everything is made of chances. We are back with Virginia Woolf: the unintentional that ends by being intentional... the flickering lights of passing moments. They are everywhere in Francis Davison's art.

And there is another light that is also always present in his collages. No matter how bright the scatter of details, Davison ensures that each enhances the glow of the whole. If you put your finger over the black spot near the middle of the lower edge of the collage to the right and imagine a full white circle, the composition as a whole doesn't blaze so brightly, though why would be impossible to describe in words. This overall 'light' is the other side of Virginia Woolf's contradiction: the elusive radiance of the everlasting present.

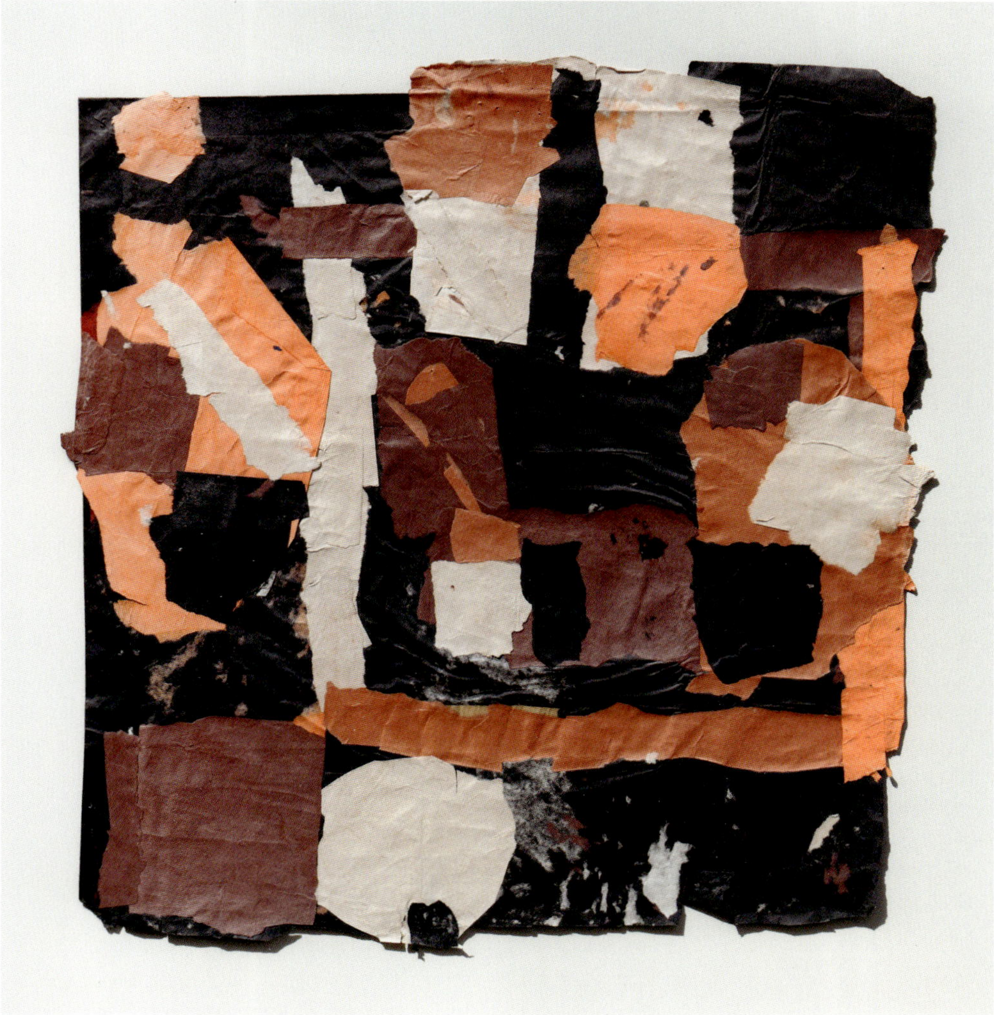

Orange, Cream and Maroon on Black, paper collage

The collages in this exhibition are all by Davison, and yet Francis himself is nowhere to be seen. He is, in a strange way, as he was in life, totally, almost furiously, self-effacing – and yet his works are entirely individual; intense, deeply felt creations, nothing else. We are left only with momentary experiences of living, which magically Davison has made lasting – to let the light shine through.

Calendar

October 2024 - 2025

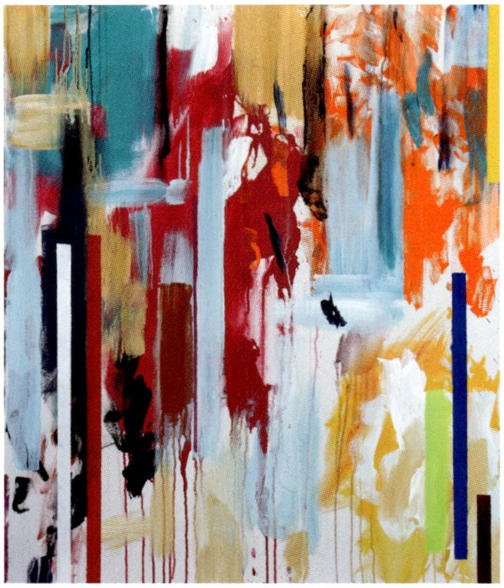

26 October Graham Boyd

When American Abstract Expressionism first arrived on these shores in the 1950s, Graham Boyd (1928-2024), who sadly passed away this summer, gladly embraced the libertine scale and dynamism of a Hans Hofmann or a Jackson Pollock. At 96, with a seven-decade career behind him, he was still painting daily in his studio, committed as ever to explorations of light, space and colour in his abstract canvases. We know that Graham was excited to be preparing work for this planned exhibition, which will now go ahead as a memorial celebration.

16 November Nic Collins

Nic Collins' is a take-no-prisoners approach to pottery: his anagama wood firings push pots (and crew) to breaking point, exposing them to an erratic flame path and temperatures reaching 1300°C. But the results are certainly worth it: astonishing beads of molten ash turned to glass, blushed surface colours, ranging from muted bluish greys to intense oranges, and ghostly imprints of fumed scallop shells. This latest exhibition – Nic's fifth at Goldmark – should come at just the right time of year: toasted pots, bearing evidence of the fire, as Winter beckons.

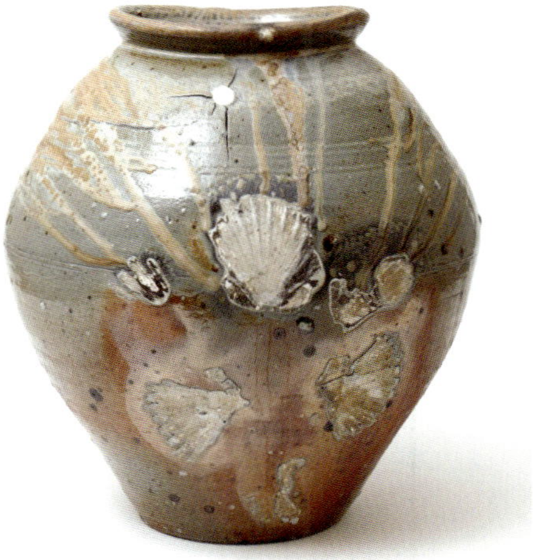

2025 Christopher P Wood Grimms Fairy Tales

It was around 25 years ago that gallery artist Christopher P. Wood held his major retrospective exhibition at the Mercer Art Gallery in Harrogate. We are delighted to announce that Chris has been invited back, this time, to showcase an ongoing labour of love reinterpreting the classic tales of the Brothers Grimm. It's a project that will be displayed in tandem with another exhibition at Mercer, exploring a wealth of pre and post-war British art with a new bequest of Neo-Romantic paintings at its core, supplemented with some exceptional loans from Goldmark. Final dates TBC.

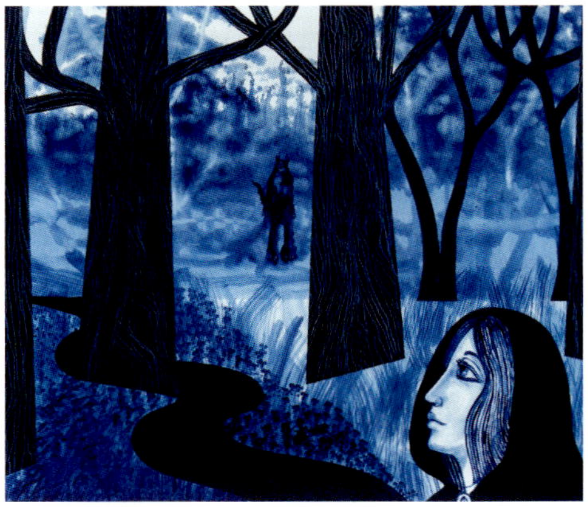

2025 Anthony Gross Book

Anthony Gross (1905-84), is still best known as our most prolific Official War Artist, and as a renowned etcher who could bring the everyday living of Paris suburbs and Lot valley vineyards vividly to life. Still unsung are his tremendous post-war oil paintings, documenting the 30 years Gross spent returning, every summer, to the village of Le Boulvé. A new book and feature-length documentary from Goldmark will shine a light on an extraordinary career still yet to be fully explored.

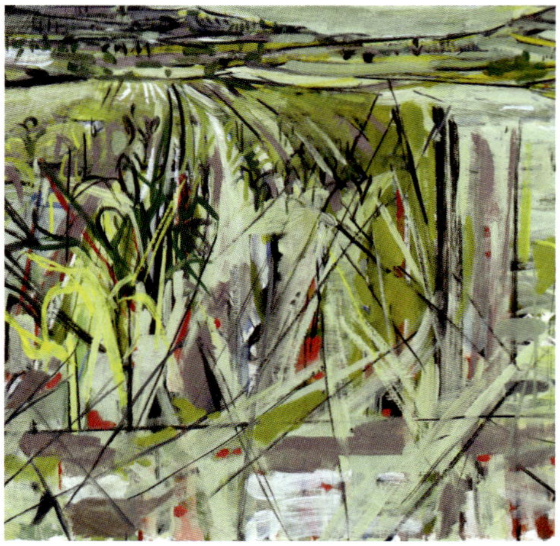